Development Anthropology

GLYNN COCHRANE

New York   OXFORD UNIVERSITY PRESS   1971

200027

To My Parents

The Kerry Cow

There was a man living in a city who had a Kerry cow. The cow had no grass and used to eat things out of the gutter. At last the owner felt sorry for this cow; he took the animal to the top of a very high mountain nearby. Driving in a stake to tether his cow on the rocky summit he said: "Well now you might not have much to eat but you'll have a grand view."

Anonymous, from a Dublin pub

Acknowledgments

The staff of Oxford University Press, New York, in particular James Raimes, have been most helpful in preparing this book for publication. My wife, an anthropologist, gave useful criticism. Raymond Noronha offered assistance at all stages. I am grateful to the Editor of the *Journal of Developing Areas* for permission to use the material in Chapter V; the Editor of the *Journal of the Polynesian Society* gave permission for material used in Chapter IV. Responsibility is, of course, entirely mine.

G. C.

Contents

Development Anthropology

I

Introduction

'Development' is an emotive term; it appeals to feeling rather than intellect. Hopes, doubts, fears, and conflicts generated by its use are not confined to citizens of new nations, they are part of the academic scene. It is important to realize that the term means different things to different people. An administrator thinks of doing things; an academic thinks of writing about things. Yes. But similarities do exist.

'Applied' anthropology, a child of colonialism in Britain, a concern with Indian affairs in the United States, involved a great deal of feeling on the part of anthropologists. The imagery —even today—is largely Victorian. Expatriates in government are 'administrators,' locals are 'backward.' But the 'jack-of-all-trades' administrator has vanished with the growth of specialization in development work. We have no accurate up-to-date account of development administration—Belshaw's *Island Administration in the South West Pacific* (1950) is badly out of date, and no anthropologist has done justice to the issues involved. 'Natives' and 'tribes' are becoming more like 'us.' 'Applied' anthropologists still think of Evans-Pritchard's government-sponsored research in the Sudan in the 1930's or Barnett's work with the United States Navy in the 1950's in the trust territories of the Pacific; a few still pose as intellectual Robin Hoods, fighting wicked administrators.[1] Since questions of what to do or how to do things require either experience of policy formation or research into the issues at a national level, which anthropologists have not usually had, the continual discussion by anthropologists of the role that they think they ought to play, unaccompanied by any appreciation of the practical requirements of the situation, is unrealistic. A modern 'applied' anthropologist in the field must now work with agriculturalists, economists, educators, public administrators, and lawyers, yet the interests and capacities of these specialists are not dealt with in anthropological literature. There is, perhaps, a need for an anthropology of 'applied' anthropology: the subject never grew and has never escaped from its colonial mold. Why?

Now that the colonial era is drawing to a close, there is not, to my knowledge, a single 'applied' anthropologist employed by the British government on 'permanent and pensionable' terms of service, i.e., on a full-time career basis. When anthropologists were engaged in the colonial territories on short-term assignments overseas, or as government anthropologists for a number of years, they obtained information that might be 'useful' to the government. It was the kind of information that could not be obtained through normal administrative channels. And the reason why anthropologists are not now regularly employed is because they do not now appear to administrators to have much to say that is useful which cannot be obtained through normal administrative channels. But for several reasons it was hard for anthropologists to make a dent on the policy-making apparatus in the colonies.[2]

Anthropology had grown under the wing of the Colonial Office in Britain, and academics were restrained when dealing

1. I do not intend here to give the entire history—most texts give this in detail. The best summary—concise and to the point—is Hogbin's survey in R. Firth (ed.), *Man and Culture: An Evaluation of the Work of Bronislaw Malinowski*, Boston, 1964.
2. René Maunier, *The Sociology of Colonies*, London, 1949, gives a good account of colonial ideology; Margery Perham, *The Colonial Reckoning*, New York, 1962, is an historical analysis; Sir Percy Cohen, *British Policy in Changing Africa*, Evanston, Illinois, 1959, puts forth the civil service viewpoint; and, for an idea of the depth of feeling involved, see Franz Fanon, *The Wretched of the Earth*, New York, 1966.

with overseas policy matters. Administrators received training in anthropology, and had a fairly good idea of limitations on its practical use; they learned the local language and kept close to the people, so that much of what the anthropologist had to say was not strange to them.

Colonial government, through lack of finances, had a fairly limited series of objectives, focusing mainly on the maintenance of law and order. In these circumstances there was not a great deal anthropology could do; and the 'applied' anthropological role comes more into perspective if one remembers the actual number of anthropologists in the field and in the universities, together with the fact that Britain by World War II had about five hundred million colonial subjects. The philosophy of development was pretty much settled, and anthropology could do little to alter it.

War was testing. During World War II anthropologists wrote handbooks about strange people for invading troops, dabbled in psychological warfare, and became ordinary civil servants. But when peace came they had not demonstrated that anthropology possessed the ability to add an indispensable dimension to the government process. They had really done no more than other bright people from the universities, the historians and the classicists.[3] And, incidentally, it is only comparatively recently that government authorities in Britain accepted that an undergraduate degree in anthropology provided an intellectual training as useful as classics or history.

The key to understanding the history of 'applied' anthropology in Britain is to keep in mind the very limited nature of the developmental objectives of the various colonial administrations and the fact that the administrative class of the civil service, both at home and overseas, was an élite. Their virtue has always been their ability to subject facts—regardless of the personal reputation of the author—to the acid test of common sense. In the same empirical tradition academics were too sensible to make extravagant claims on behalf of an 'applied' science; the major intellectual challenge was not thought to lie in this area.[4]

3. Based on conversations with British anthropologists and civil servants.
4. E. E. Evans-Pritchard, "Applied Anthropology," *Africa*, vol. 16 (1946).

However, the situation was different in America. The United States became a colonial power in the Pacific after World War II.

American administration was more loosely structured and never concentrated power in the hands of an administrative élite as in Britain; [5] people believed in specialization; civil servants stood more in awe of the academic. Apparently, there was a belief that a man with a Ph.D. should be useful in the governing of overseas territories.

Certainly American 'applied' anthropologists seem to have made more impact on the war scene than their counterparts in Britain.[6]

In the Pacific, American anthropologists found themselves wielding great power under wartime conditions. They were responsible for development planning.[7] Unfortunately, these men, who knew little other than anthropology, whose previous experience of the Pacific had been limited to fairly remote communities, fostered an anthropological 'omniscience' which planned and executed without requests for the advice of administrators or other social scientists. After this heady experience it must have been sobering and frustrating to work for the Navy on various small Pacific islands.[8] Cornell University's Vicos project, which I mention later, was a logical culmination of this.

The key to understanding American 'applied' anthropology lies in understanding the incredibly generous objectives of American foreign aid. The policy was going full speed after World War II at a time when the United States had few people with experience of development administration. The United States Navy in the Pacific had no experience in these matters and did not know what anthropology could or ought to do. United States foundations and universities went in for develop-

5. See D. Waldo, *The Study of Public Administration*, New York, 1961.
6. Foster, *Applied Anthropology*, Boston, 1969, pp. 34–36.
7. D. L. Oliver (ed.), *Planning Micronesia's Future: A Summary of the United States Commercial Company's Economic Survey of Micronesia*, Cambridge, Mass., 1946; J. Unseem, "Governing the Occupied Areas of the South Pacific: Wartime Lessons and Peacetime Proposals," *Applied Anthropology*, vol. 4, no. 3 (1945).
8. See Barnett, *Anthropology in Administration*, Evanston, 1956, p. 49.

ment in a big way. The sheer size, weight, and power of the American academic machine drove anthropology toward an 'applied' mission. The tragedy was that early American 'applied' anthropologists never really understood what development work was all about or could be all about. For most of them 'government' was a naval administrator. There was no administrative officer class, as in Britain, to say that what academics thought was 'applied' anthropology was in fact common sense or sound administration. Working with any government meant, to applied anthropologists in the universities, an unjustifiable loss of academic freedom.

The Ya-Yiront and 'cargo cult' activity [9] helped anthropologists in the United States and Britain believe that modernization was tremendously complex, 'scientific,' and understood only by anthropologists. Development gradually became community development—an exclusively anthropological process.[10]

In the United States there is an applied anthropological establishment. Anyone who wishes to say something about development work must work within the establishment's definition of the subject and must also compete over its literary obstacle course. The course contains one poorly designed fence we could name 'community development.' The course stewards removed other fences named 'economic theory,' 'legal and constitutional analyses,' and 'public administration' though few spectators understand quite why.

A leading applied anthropologist listening to a paper of mine indicated that there was a vast amount of literature on the subject and that I should go through the 'scholarly process.' I still have not read it all and am not going to. As a former professional administrator I do not always find the insights of amateur administrators posing as applied anthropologists very helpful; and, I have no intention of reading more bad and boring anthropology than necessary. Academic defense mechanisms, in the best gamesmanship tradition, are: to mention 'rigor and sys-

9. D. G. Cochrane, *Big Men and Congo Cults,* Oxford, 1970.
10. See, for example, Goodenough, *Cooperation in Change,* New York, 1963; Foster, *Applied Anthropology; Traditional Cultures: And the Impact of Technological Change,* New York, 1962.

tematic analysis,' which means, sheer boredom; or, what some 'big name' has said, which means that if a graduate student had submitted the work to a professional journal it would not have been published. One can be polemical about administrators but not about the establishment. For applied anthropologists there can be few things more alarming than common sense.

But, then, for many anthropologists few things are more alarming than applied anthropology.

When the West declared a 'war on want' in the 1950's, anthropologists were not in the front line. Instead newly emergent countries found themselves with chairs of social work, staffed by people whose fieldwork was done in Brooklyn or Boston; [11] sociologists and political scientists made themselves useful; [12] economists became the high priests of development. Anthropologists did not effectively protest the fact that their discipline was ignored. Today there are fewer anthropologists in the international agencies than ever before.[13] Much of the responsibility for this can be traced to the fact that extravagant claims were not backed by results. (Incidentally, I concentrate on rural development though I do not attempt to do justice to vital issues like population control, education, and agriculture.)

Applied anthropology has not been scholarly or academic, though sensitivity on this matter is understandable. You may search in vain through all the books on applied anthropology for a comment on international aid giving, or on the policies of the United Nations and its associated agencies. What you will find will be a series of community development projects, distinguished only by their similarity and almost complete lack of importance. Read one episode: you have read them all. To develop a country on this basis—indeed to get anything accomplished

11. The universities in Zambia and Tanzania, for example, had, in 1967, no anthropology staff though they did have chairs of social work and social administration.

12. While anthropologists concern themselves with the problems of the community, sociologists and political scientists concern themselves with national issues. See, for example, the special issue of *The Administrative Science Quarterly*, December 1968, devoted to the design of development bureaucracies.

13. Foster, *Applied Anthropology*, p. 217.

—would require thousands and thousands of anthropologists. Even then there would probably be little coordination.

The issues in applied anthropology—to do or not to do—are for personal decision. But at a time when anthropological knowledge is badly needed in the emerging nations there is little justification for moralizing to the extent that nothing gets done. No doubt there are plenty of people who will raise all sorts of objections to show how mistaken I am; metaphysical debate has become a minor industry in applied anthropology. We have too many Utopians. Development or modernization has never been painless and never will be. It carries a fairly heavy social price tag. There is no sense in creating an anthropological Utopia and then criticizing the inevitable shortfalls.

The sociology of the *total* society in emerging countries has been ignored. Anthropologists have hardly ever felt it necessary to take a *professional* interest—as opposed to making value judgments and voicing political opinions—in the expatriate class. Could anyone deny that, as far as colonial territories were concerned, the 'science of man' was simply the science of *some* men? Preferably 'native'?

It is unfortunate that the American Anthropological Association has not adopted a more forward role toward international development policy. This is an odd omission in view of the criticism of colonialist policies offered by individual anthropologists. The omission of anthropology from the international agency scene could legitimately have been protested by the association. Ironically, the association itself has also been in the early colonial mold, being content to maintain internal law and order. Other national anthropological societies and associations have done no better.

Anthropology is taught in graduate schools with the primary aim of producing recruits for the academic system. This is important, but the most important thing in development work is not simply to write about things but also to achieve progress or results on the ground. Applied anthropologists have stressed *writing* about things. What has been achieved in applied anthropology, given the agonizing problems that people face—hunger, disease, overpopulation, and sickness—in various parts of the world? Very little. Applied anthropologists are not involved in development programs to any great extent, and those in which they are involved tend to be part time. These issues merit something more than a part-time approach.

But many international agencies and governments do not now need applied anthropologists—at least that is the impression I have received. They have Spicer's, Goodenough's, and Arensberg and Niehoff's work. These applied anthropology texts tell 'how-to-do-it' and imply that people can become amateur anthropologists by reading these books. Professionals are redundant. These books have done anthropology a very great disservice. It is illogical to talk about ethics and professionalism while applied texts attempt to turn Everyman into an amateur anthropologist. Difficulties are minimized; solutions appear too easy.

I would like to see an entirely new approach. I argue in this book that there are cogent reasons for objection to the subject as it is presently conceived. On neither practical nor intellectual grounds is there any good reason to be sympathetic toward applied anthropology and its advocates. It has been sterile and unimaginative for too long; it is not a respectable subject in academic circles, though it is usually studied by people who have doctorates. It would be surely logical to harness for this work all those students who have got as far as an M.A. in anthropology but who do not wish to spend their days in university life. Can we not offer them such a career?

I have many friends in academic life who are scornful indeed of the kinds of things that applied anthropology has been doing, but often they do not sufficiently appreciate that it is not the development problems themselves which are inherently bad but the way in which they have been tackled. The solution of problems is an academic process. But the implementation of plans— doing things and being involved—is also a vital part of applied anthropology; it is not an academic process though it must still rely on academic analysis. The new nations and their problems are not to be considered merely as an extension of a university department, which seems to be how they are regarded in the applied anthropology literature.

One of my strong feelings about development is just this: that problems are created by the way we approach things as much as by the attitudes, beliefs, and values of those we seek to help. I stress throughout this book that although anthropology provides a good and useful way to look at things, a variety of approaches are usually necessary; anthropologists, administrators, and other social scientists who are concerned with these problems should get to know more about each others' work. This is the knowledge that applied anthropologists should have had over and above their conventional training.

Interdisciplinary work has not been very successful; things can only improve if it becomes clear that interdisciplinary researchers gain insights which are more valuable than those obtained within a single social science discipline. At present, people go in for broadly based studies because they are not very competent in any single discipline; or a number of scholars contribute to a volume, each presenting the viewpoint of his own discipline and the result being termed 'interdisciplinary.' The essence of interdisciplinary work must surely be the overview, a process that demands and requires the individual researchers to have competence in several fields. For the anthropologist who is interested in development problems this is a *must*.

My concern is to show that we have not made much progress with applied anthropology, to show the awfully long way we must still go before anything useful can be brought into being and sustained, and to suggest new approaches and ways of looking at things that might be profitable. There is bias involved. Having been an administrator-anthropologist for seven years, I know how useful anthropological advice can be and how badly it is needed. To remark here on something I will repeat in one of the following chapters: if things do not work out properly it is not because disciplines and professions are antagonistic to each other but because their attitudes are. I am myself fairly quarrelsome in the pages that follow, but I could think of no other way to highlight the fact that anthropology's potential contribution has not even begun to be realized. To account for this I go deeply into the traditional concerns of applied anthropologists, their dislike of administrators and their belief in community development. It seems to me there has been a desire to interject some of the concerns governments have about small-scale development projects into anthropological literature. I would like to see individual anthropologists become policymakers at the national level. I think we have to create a general practitioner class with anthropological training and familiarity with other disciplines that impinge on development work. These people should do a government or international agency internment to appreciate the practical consequences of and opportunities offered by such a career.

Where these people work in an organization setting then their first loyalty must be to that agency or government, and they must be prepared to accept that other professionals may know more about some things than they do and that it may be a long, slow, and frustrating process before the value of an anthropological training is fully appreciated. Nothing could be more dangerous or stultifying than to look at problems from the perspective of one's own discipline alone and to fail to realize that anthropology is only a part, albeit a vital part, of the total scheme of things in development work. There is truth in the maxim, "the tail doesn't wag the dog."

For anthropologists, applied anthropology has been bad anthropology; to administrators it has been bad administration; it has as yet made insufficient impact on other disciplines and professions involved in development work. Things must change. This book is directed toward students and teachers of anthropology and toward authorities charged with the planning and execution of development programs. I believe that there is increasing disenchantment with the kinds of practical contribution made by anthropology, and while I do not hope to 'turn around' applied work it may be that the raising of these questions will prompt some people to take a personal initiative. But only when universities, international agencies, and governments, acting in concert, initiate the necessary training programs will significant progress be made. Anthropology has to begin to train for export as well as for domestic consumption.

II

Some Science of Some Men
and Some Problems

Articles of the 'Administration and Anthropology' type have been written mainly by academics with no personal experience of administration in the developing countries. Nor have these amateur public administrators bothered to familiarize themselves with the analytical approach or concerns of students of public administration. It might be helpful, even equitable, to write from the administrative viewpoint for a change.

To show that the applied anthropologist's work is neither sound anthropology nor sensible public administration I examine three books, and in part focus on Dr. Thompson's paper, "Is Applied Anthropology Helping To Develop a Science of Man?" (1965), since it encapsulates much of the essence of recent thinking in applied anthropology.

I question whether existing approaches do show that applied anthropologists can play a useful role in development work. The claim to professionalism in development work is dubious and no sound theory on the prediction or production of social change has as yet emerged. Failures to analyze development administration scientifically, a lack of scholarly attention paid to other disciplines and professions which impinge on the development

scene (apart from community development) and a poor record
of cooperation with other professionals demand a more realistic
appreciation of what is required in development work than additional projects conceived, executed, and evaluated by applied
anthropologists themselves.

Cooperation in Change by W. H. Goodenough, *Human Problems in Technological Change*, edited by E. H. Spicer, and *Introducing Social Change* by C. M. Arensberg and A. H. Niehoff,
raise issues which make it difficult to accept that applied anthropology is a sound profession.

There are three important features in development work. The
first is a knowledge of the local culture, the second, a sophisticated knowledge based on analysis and study of other areas and
trends, covering all aspects of development, i.e., what might be
done, the third, a knowledge of how to implement plans. The
applied anthropologist might be competent in terms of the first
category. The second category has not been stressed and demands intensive academic analysis over and above traditional
anthropological knowledge—in development economics, tropical agriculture, and law, for instance. The third category again
requires academic analysis, and experience. The applied anthropologist who has neglected categories two and three is really
not very much more useful than a knowledgeable member of the
community he studies. But in fact these books are addressed to
people who will not even have competence in the first category,
i.e., they are addressed to nonanthropologists who will not have
a scientific knowledge of the local culture.

Spicer claims (p. 13) that the applied anthropologist's responsibilities are even greater than those of a surgeon. A. H. Leighton, writing the foreword to Goodenough's book, says: "Although
the author points out that his work is not a 'how-to-do-it' book
—not a Baedeker for the cross cultural traveller—it is important
to note that it contains innumerable points of practical guidance
and suggestions that are readily translatable into action." Goodenough's own disclaimer is hard to accept when we come across
this (p. 372): "The degree to which new rules find acceptance
and voluntary compliance depends directly on how well they

meet the conditions we have outlined." Arensberg and Niehoff make no bones about their contribution (p. 9): "The main function of this book is to instill an approach, a sensitivity, an inventiveness and a set of principles for cultural solution of such problems. Primarily it can show the agent his main challenge: to search out and find the local customs into which his innovations can be best blended." It is doubtful if the American Medical Association would encourage all United States citizens abroad to act in similar vein.

Applied anthropology is obviously one of the few professions for which no professional training is required. These books contain little more than common textbook anthropology. If they simply tried to teach anthropology this would be admirable. However, the layman is given to understand that if he can grasp and apply 'cultural principles' then his goals will more easily be achieved.

Most professionals have to live with and account for their mistakes. Applied anthropologists are more fortunate. If their hit-or-miss methods do not work, they can always move on to new pastures. As Foster says: "From the standpoint of scientific research, failure or success of a particular project is incidental . . . It is unfortunately true that most of the readings in the field of applied anthropology are analyses of failures or partial failures." [1] It is instructive to examine a little more closely the way applied anthropologists predict and produce social change.

Dr. Thompson discusses a method of clinical prediction. Mention is made of an "if. . . . . then" proposition. H. G. Barnett said: "There seems to be no reason for assuming that a human being is more difficult to understand or control than is an atom . . . For this reason in anthropology as in physics, a regularity, hence a prediction, is properly phrased in the conditional tense: if A happens B is likely to follow." [2] Although this is the goal which social scientists are working toward, it is not an accurate representation of the present position—our methods of measure-

1. *Traditional Cultures: And the Impact of Technological Change*, New York, 1962, pp. 232–234.
2. "Anthropology as an Applied Science," *Human Organization*, xvii, no. 1 (1958).

ment and instrumentation are still unsophisticated, as Karl Popper has pointed out:

The Social Sciences know nothing that can be compared to the mathematically formulated causal laws of Physics . . . the causal laws of the social sciences, supposing that there are any, must differ widely from those of Physics, being qualitative rather than quantitative and mathematical . . . It appears that qualities—whether physical or non-physical—can only be appraised by intuition." [3]

Dr. Thompson says (my emphasis): "the applied anthropologist usually employs a clinical method which *is as yet inadequately understood.* It is based on understanding in depth of the changing culture of a community in historic and geographic perspective, including the community's covert attitudes and implicit values. Frequently the method involves knowledge of the community's unconscious group personality or psychic system. It also demands a refined concept of culture as an emergent out of the past with direction into the future, and specification of an activity unit of analysis as significant in relation to the scientific problem." Dr. Thompson is rather diffident about this theory which must be of fundamental interest to all social scientists. We are referred to Goodenough's book where he "attempts to explain what is involved."

Goodenough says of his book: "It does not attempt to provide a detailed theory of social change . . . Theory of change is not yet scientifically mature (p. 30) . . . knowledge of the processes of social change is still sketchy (p. 24)." However, later, he says (p. 323): "Even within the limitations of present knowledge a fair degree of prediction and intelligent direction of the course of change is possible." Goodenough informs the layman (pp. 346–347): "For development agents it is a safe rule that insofar as it is possible to solve a client community's problems by utilizing its established institutions, the solution is more likely to make sense to the community's members and not strike them as threatening . . . Where the problem cannot be solved in this manner but requires change in the community's institutional structure, agents may anticipate that, whatever solution is

3. *The Poverty of Historicism,* New York, 1964, pp. 25, 26.

adopted a number of new problems are likely to arise in conse-quence." This seems a fairly casual approach. If Peace Corps workers for instance are to be given the tools to promote inno-vation, and if they are to be able to overcome local resistance,[4] then surely they will require something a little more lucid than a clinical method which, as Dr. Thompson says, is "as yet inade-quately understood" by professional anthropologists.

Applied anthropologists do not live in the harsh world of reality where claims to predict or produce change must be backed by results. They like to evaluate their own results. The applied anthropologist has two roles. He is good at drilling wells, branding cows, and persuading people to take pills. And, he educates his countrymen going overseas.

In Spicer's book, each of its case studies merely illustrates some administrative skills backed by superficial local knowl-edge. Its method of analysis resembles the well-known case method of the Harvard Business School or the forecasting of a business corporation. There is no anthropological analysis, noth-ing other than the vague reference to principles, beliefs, and values different from our own. The studies in Spicer's text are really based on intuition and opinion and in my view the unsuc-cessful cases show a woeful lack of administrative competence on the part of those who attempted to introduce changes.

Applied anthropologists have been kind to themselves, as usual, in evaluating the Vicos project. "The community re-sponded remarkably; and Holmberg's experiment proved an im-portant point not only for anthropology but also for the people of Vicos and Peru, for all others in similar circumstances, and for the policy making powers in the world." [5] The significance of Vicos was not brought home to me when I was in government service though I think any administrator would be unfair if he did not express admiration for those who handled the public re-lations side of the Vicos project.

4. None of these authors seriously question the rectitude of innovation. It is assumed that any Peace Corps worker (or businessman in the case of Arensberg and Niehoff) is quite entitled to produce changes.
5. S. Tax, "The Uses of Anthropology" in J. D. Jennings and E. A. Hoebel, *Readings in Anthropology*, New York, 1966.

This experiment set and achieved goals. For this reason change is held to have been directed and controlled. The kinds of results which were obtained were no more spectacular than those achieved by nonanthropologists in community development projects all over the world. The anthropological set-up at Vicos was a minute government. All governments set goals, many of which are achieved. Here again, as in Spicer's case, the applied anthropologist exercises some administrative skills and claims that what he is doing is applied anthropology—a kind of transubstantiation through jargon.[6] Did this project have implications for large-scale development schemes?

Vicos shows an absence of any real appreciation of what development work is all about. At Vicos the anthropologist apparently made all the major decisions. No competent administrator would himself deal with agricultural, legal, and educational matters since these are specialized subjects which require expert assessment and advice. Through consultation among specialist members of a development team, including an anthropologist, policy can be decided. Vicos shows the kind of anthropologist who believes that he knows all he needs to know about development, and who does not feel the need to cooperate with other disciplines except on a very cursory basis. Vicos was small. There have been many outstanding community development projects whose architects have shown a greater awareness of the need for teamwork, and who have been a little more restrained in awarding themselves prizes.

The process of persuading people in the developing countries to adopt new techniques is not new. Extension workers rely on their own experience, judgment, knowledge of local circumstances, and the fact that they have earned the confidence of the people. These workers have a corpus of knowledge which is more comprehensive and useful than anything Vicos has produced. Do applied anthropologists really think, and their writing suggests they do, that they are the first people to achieve any

6. See A. R. Holmberg, "The Research and Development Approach to the Study of Change," *Human Organization*, XVII, no. 1 (1958).

kind of success on these problems?[7] Projects like Vicos are a prime reason for administrative failure to use anthropologists because what the latter term 'science' is simply a matter of common knowledge.

The world of the applied anthropologist is made up of communities. A few he can attend to personally. Others he leaves to the only other kind of person who inhabits his world, the development agent. Community development appears, like Vicos, as a process of one man taking all the important decisions. Goodenough seems to think that problems at the community level are the same as those problems found at the national level because, incredibly, he stretches his definition of community to include a nation (p. 16). There is not time, in view of the urgent problems the developing nations face, to await community mapping of an entire nation. There is not time to wait for restudies. Applied anthropologists must attempt much more than they have done to make their specialty inform those concerned with national policy. This is a theoretical challenge.

A community development project, especially one with a low technical input like Vicos, cannot normally form an adequate basis for national planning. Vicos was a very expensive public relations project for applied anthropology. How has this project helped Peru, all others in similar circumstances, and the policy-making powers of the world? We must now, for a change, have an evaluation from an independent source. A little of Dr. Thompson's rigorous empiricism is required. If applied anthropology had really been analytical, academic inquiry would have broadened these very narrow concerns.

Applied anthropologists often stress that they need the respect of their academic colleagues. They often fail to mention that they must also earn the respect of other professionals in a development situation. Those whose business is the science of human relations are sometimes personally deficient in such matters.

7. See Foster, *Traditional Cultures*, ix–xiii; Goodenough, *Cooperation*, pp. 21–22. The suggestion is that development work was very imprecise until the anthropologists came along and that they are now playing (or are capable of playing) a major role in development work.

Dr. Thompson's paper cannot resist casting aspersions on the impartiality and competence of administrators. "Success . . . will be measured by the empirical test, not . . . administrators' prejudices and preferences . . . Despite the carefully worded Charter it is reported that persistent and often unwitting attempts on the part of the administrators occurred to maneuver the anthropologists into a position of endorsing and advocating goals or ends to be sought." Many applied anthropologists have commented in similar vein.[8] The anthropological viewpoint has certainly not changed since the famous exchanges between Mitchell and Malinowski,[9] and, as Foster pointed out, we still have no study of a development bureaucracy.[10]

This kind of writing does not contribute to the establishment of better working relationships in the field. Such criticism pays insufficient attention to Geoffrey Wilson's sound advice: "The scientists must make it their boast that both Governments and oppositions can trust them equally because they say nothing that they cannot prove, because they are pedestrian and never leave the facts." [11] Dr. Lucy Mair has also commented: "Certainly inadequately informed assertions about the aims and methods of the emissaries of Western culture do nothing to enhance the value of a field work report." [12] Existing comment on administrators is mostly very bad anthropological thinking.

The dispute between anthropologists and administrators can be traced to Malinowski, who is recognized by Thompson as the founder of applied anthropology (Goodenough dedicated his book to Malinowski). Although Malinowski recognized the need

8. See H. G. Barnett, *Anthropology in Administration*, Evanston, 1956, pp. 59, 69; C. J. Erasmus, *Man Takes Control*, Minneapolis, 1961, pp. 163–166; W. H. Goodenough, *Cooperation*, p. 432; A. H. Leighton, *Human Relations in a Changing World*, New York, 1949, p. 148; S. Tax, "Anthropology and Administration," *American Indigena*, XI (1945).

9. B. Malinowski, "Practical Anthropology," *Africa*, vol. II, no. 1, 1929, and P. E. Mitchell, "The Anthropologist and the Practical Man," *Africa*, vol. II, no. 2., 1930.

10. Foster, *Applied Anthropology*, pp. 91, 92.

11. G. Wilson, "Anthropology as a Public Service," *Africa*, XIII, no. I (1940).

12. *Methods of Study of Culture Contact in Africa*, International Institute of African Languages and Cultures 1938.

for research on expatriates living in the developing countries, he made little progress on this, and to him, perhaps, we owe the start of a rather tactless and unscientific stream of value judgments. If anthropologists had studied administrators in a scholarly way—applied anthropologists inform us that even factory managements can be so studied [13]—then their strictures would be more palatable.

Dr. Mair (p. 237) has commented on Malinowski's advice to the modern ethnographer that he must be "acquainted with the sociology of western enterprise, political, economic, and educational," saying that "field work on Europeans in Africa, however, is still confined to the type recommended by Fortes and Schapera, in which the local representatives of European culture are observed as 'integrally part of the community'—that is to say, as persons in daily interaction with them, whose presence and activities are taken for granted."

But in his work on the Trobriands, Malinowski had not adopted his own advice, and in his introduction to *Methods of Study of Culture Contact in Africa* (see p. ix), he adopted the kind of uninformed condescension toward expatriates which has continued. The contact student would be adequately prepared if he read "a dozen or so of books on native policies, education, economics, and on missionary programmes (xvii, fn.)." Goodenough has made the same point as Malinowski (p. 26) and the same mistake.

Essentially Goodenough believes (p. 429) that administration can be characterized as a cycle which includes the following activities: A, Decision-making; B, Programming; C, Communicating; D, Controlling; E, Reappraising. He would reduce anthropology in the same fashion to: A, Collection of data; B, Analysis of data; C, Comparison of data; D, Communication; E, Reappraisal. Goodenough builds up a picture of development administration by taking completely out of context random examples from industry or a metropolitan civil service. On page 442 he gives us an example from the British civil service, and on the next page an example from a United States steel corporation. Later he

13. See E. D. Chapple, "Anthropological Engineering: Its Use to Administrators," *Applied Anthropology*, II, no. 2 (1943).

moves to the Gilberts. Administrators, according to Goodenough, are rather nasty people who will do anything to get ahead
(pp. 444–445), and they can be contrasted with the more lofty
situation of the academic. The criticisms which Goodenough
makes about administrators have been made by Erasmus about
academics.[14] If applied anthropologists wish to continue to wave
their academic flag, then we are entitled to see a scholarly analysis of the literature in the field of public administration.

There is a very great difference between civil service functions in a complex society and development administration. Personnel, training, roles, and objectives are worlds apart. Who the
administrators are or what positions they occupy is seldom
made clear by any applied anthropologist. This kind of bias and
inaccuracy is inexcusable when an anthropologist sets himself
up as an expert on development work. Obviously these mistakes
stem from inadequate personal experience or scholarly analysis
of development administration.

Applied anthropologists in the United States have had contact
with administrators employed by the international agencies such
as W.H.O (who usually have received little specialized training
for development work), or the U.S. trust territories where, in the
postwar years, owing to inexperience, there was little administrative knowledge,[15] or A.I.D. This is not really sufficient experience on which to make the kind of broad generalizations that
applied anthropologists have made. Goodenough's lack of
method and rather obvious bias against administrators come
through clearly when he says (p. 432): "Automation now brings
the administrators' ideal one step closer to fruition by presum-
ably eliminating operators entirely, leaving none but the maintenance man between the administrative programmer and the
machine. The pushbutton world may not inappropriately be labelled the administrators' utopia." Goodenough has confused his
experience of university administration with development ad-

14. Erasmus, *Man Takes Control*, pp. 160–163; and see also R. Ross's
comment on p. 433 in A. W. Gouldner and S. M. Miller (eds.), *Applied Sociology*, New York, 1965.
15. This is made clear by H. C. Barnett's *Anthropology in Administration*,
Evanston, 1956.

ministration. He gave a more accurate account of development administration when he said (p. 386): "Like Colonial administrators in the Gilberts he must work to put himself out of a job. To do this, he must play progressively different and progressively less important roles in the community's affairs."

Applied anthropologists have not done their homework on this question. And if applied anthropologists do not take the trouble to find out how governments work or operate, then it is hard to see on what basis they could presume to make policy recommendations.

The nature of any administration will be unique. Its essential features cannot be described or appreciated unless it is given the same patient attention that other institutions in the developing world receive from anthropologists. Certainly existing approaches show little of Dr. Thompson's 'scientific maturity.'

Cooperation in Change is an ironic title for a book which does not advocate cooperation with other disciplines. Few applied anthropologists have had any specialized training in other disciplines which impinge on the development field. Applied anthropologists seem to think that any series of lectures on culture will meet the bill. The transition from one or two years' experience in a remote community to expert status on development work is quite an awesome *rite de passage*.

We have yet to see anthropologists mount any serious attack on the very inflated role of the economist in planning development work. While some anthropologists argue over the meaning of economics, or construct new dynamic models to explain minute events, economists propose constraints on nations in an attempt to force them to conform to the Western development model.[16]

A distinction has yet to be made—and it must be made—between producing social change and enabling social change to take place. It seems more logical that the role of the applied anthropologist should be that of the midwife rather than, as Arensberg and Niehoff (p. 6) and Spicer suggest, that of the

16. J. S. G. Wilson, *An Economic Survey of the New Hebrides*, London, 1965.

surgeon. Applied anthropologists keep mentioning 'science' though there is nothing, as I have said, very scientific about their analysis of development problems. People in charge of development work are not going to come to terms with anthropology: Things must be the other way around. It seems naïve of anthropologists to attempt to show that cultural change can be produced by laymen, to cast aspersions without any scientific basis on administrators, and then to end up with pleas for employment.

III

Development Anthropology:
A New Name, A New Approach

The concept of an 'applied' science is a continuing source of internecine strife among anthropologists. When I consider the vast literature, largely polemical, dealing with applied anthropology, much of it devoted to the question of whether or not such knowledge can be *applied,* or denial of the existence of a 'pure' as opposed to an 'applied' science. I sense that the designation applied is itself a major handicap to establishment of a more peaceful anthropological community. A number of anthropologists with an applied like orientation call their work plain 'anthropology' rather than risk the appellation applied.

This is an embarrassment apparently suffered only by anthropologists among the social sciences (and sociologists to a lesser extent); economists and political scientists have a more pragmatic approach, and their equivalent of applied is not, as far as I can see, a resting place for second-class citizens.

We might make a similar impact on academic sensibilities if we were to create a 'Protestant,' a 'Catholic,' or a 'Jewish' anthropology. The term 'applied anthropology' is not itself strictly correct. It is erroneous to suggest that when, for example, an anthropologist is undertaking socio-economic research, he is applying anthropological knowledge alone. He also applies knowledge of economic theory. However, ironically, it is the very attempt to apply anthropological knowledge alone which, in my opinion, has been largely responsible for failure to make progress. A man who can apply only anthropological knowledge is never going to be very useful in a development situation.

A major difficulty with applied anthropology is its promise to *do*. And obviously a good deal of the work done in the 'applied' area is not going to be used to *do* anything but is simply collected for its own intrinsic value as a part of an ongoing scientific process. Two functions are unforgivably mixed up under the 'applied' umbrella. Analysis and study of problems belongs in academia; doing things, giving advice, taking action, on the basis of university training and in the light of personal experience is the professional role of a general practitioner.

The character of anthropology has been determined by the nature of the problem that academics were interested in and the kinds of intellectual inquiry deemed necessary to reach an adequate level of understanding. The subject achieved a certain unity because a number of people chose similar kinds of problems and there was some broad measure of agreement about how these should be tackled. But in development work things are a little different. The problems will not, so often, be those that interest the academic but rather those suggested by the exigencies of the situation as it appears to authorities. And one must be prepared to redefine anthropology—its traditional boundaries have been more a matter of academic convenience than scholarly logic.

Many applied anthropologists feel that their role is determined by 'science.' The Ethical Code of the Society for Applied Anthropology even says that one has a duty to science. *What* I do is a human problem, *how* I do something may have something to do with scientific method. I have no duty to science though I do feel an obligation to my fellow men. Applied anthropology has always had a distinctly ideological tinge, a pale tincturing of academic narcissism, and a comforting view of the world and the applied man's place in it.

Applied anthropology has never succeeded in separating ques-tions of science from personal values—and values are not the subject of an exact science.[1] Confusion is bound to arise in advi-sory work because giving advice, forming policy, and guiding change are all kinds of activity involved with choice. Two ele-ments are involved in the decision-making of applied anthropolo-gists: (a) selection of a set of alternatives to choose from, (b) selection of a set of preferences to rank the alternatives against.[2] The best solution or course of action is a matter of personal opinion rather than scientific fact. The applied anthropologist cannot claim to have *the* scientific way to guide change; he should not be allowed to misrepresent personal opinion under a guise of science. Where public issues are concerned the applied anthropologist has no scientific way to measure distribution ben-efits.[3] It is a dangerous step, too often taken, to move from being aware that one knows more about a people's culture than anyone else to believing and advocating that one also knows what is best for the people.

I think we have to admit that it was naïve to even attempt to establish a science of means to deal with human distress, social change, or any of the traditional concerns of applied anthropol-ogy. A science of means might be a possible endeavor in a very stable social environment in which all effective political ele-ments accept a common ideology, common authority, and a

1. Donald Kingsley quoted in Redford, *Ideal and Practice in Public Administration*, Birmingham, Alabama, 1958, p. 31.
2. R. A. Bauer and K. J. Gergen (eds.), *The Study of Policy Formation*, New York, 1968, pp. 68, 69. This study sensibly points out that "any opti-mised model for decision making (a model for the best solution) is built around the notion that some preference scheme can be established accord-ing to which the solution is optimal" (p. 12). However, there is no such thing as an optimal public policy, and this observation has significant im-plications for an 'applied' social science. For example there is no 'scientific' way that an applied anthropologist could assess educational requirements of a developing nation. What criteria is he to adopt? Education of the greatest number? What about the syllabus? Kathleen Gough Aberle's well-known statement—"Who is to evaluate and suggest guidelines for human society, if not those who study it?"—seems to me to be dangerously naïve.
3. On distributive values see, for example, H. A. Simon, *Administrative Be-havior*, New York, 1961 ed., p. 178.

common scale of values, i.e., in a Utopia! Meanwhile, anthropology may show *a* way but it will not indicate in any infallible manner *the* way.

Creation of a new designation and role to replace applied anthropology is necessary. In terms of role, technique, and method of operation, a distinction has to be made between the academic anthropology where scholars may specialize in development problems, and the anthropologist as a general practitioner or adviser in the service of a government or international agency.

Does it really matter what we call our particular specialty since all human behavior comes under the anthropological umbrella? I think it does, because of the very vastness of the subject. First, a subdisciplinary title supplies a focal point for collection, collation, and mustering of kinds of knowledge and people interested in particular types of research. No matter how much we dislike the thought it is inevitable that such emphasis will occur because some degree of specialization seems necessary. Second, use of a title should encourage familiarity with the kinds of problems encountered and the ways in which anthropologists have attempted to undertake research. Third, it is essential that the title stress a need for growth, both of the anthropologist and his specialty, through a call for more cooperation with other social sciences. In other words the name must convey something of a philosophy or orientation underlying the research into our specialty. 'Economic' anthropology and 'medical' anthropology do this accurately. The old designation 'applied' cannot meet these needs.

If we examine any textbook dealing with applied anthropology—and Foster's latest book, *Applied Anthropology*, Boston, 1969, is a good example—there is talk of 'economic development,' of 'innovating bureaucracy,' and of 'agriculture,' but no rigorous or systematic attempt to find what the experts in these fields have said.[4] We do not need any more anecdotes about community development. We do need urgently a rigorous and systematic analysis of what other disciplines have to offer

4. See for example, Mr. Pearsall, "From The Editor," *Human Organization*, XXV, no. 3 (1966), pp. 185–186, reviewing past contributions.

and a better idea of what they need from anthropology. Economists are not overly impressed by community schemes.[5]

We now recognize more and more, particularly in the emergent countries, that there are not a series of modernization problems which can be neatly delegated and dealt with by sociology, economics, or anthropology as the case may be, but that there are just problems which require the combined intellectual equipment of a number of social sciences if they are to be understood. An applied anthropologist could only have become more effective to the extent that he recognized the needs, capacities, and specialties of specific governments and international agencies.

It should be a challenge to work in areas where demand for theory is greatest—problems should not become less respectable simply because they have not been solved. All anthropologists are concerned with the question of how and why change takes place; it is only our own idiosyncrasy which would make us label one kind of inquiry scholarly and another unscholarly. The anthropological community should not be divided because of a difference in the kinds of problems that attract the interest of anthropologists, rather it should be divided because of *the way* that these problems are tackled. And if concepts and ideas are taken from other social sciences, as is the case with economic anthropology, then these techniques ought to be judged on their scientific rather than their emotional appeal.

In this book I am arguing for two things: first, for the creation of a truly academic anthropology of development; second, for the creation of a class of general practitioner anthropologists. If academic anthropology is to have policy-making implications then in the context of my previous criticisms of applied anthropology a number of positive recommendations can be made. The widest range of facts must be analyzed and alternatives exposed. And even though the demands of development work will be severe, the final decision must still rest with those charged by

5. See, for example, E. E. Hagen on the Vicos project, *The Economics of Development*, Cambridge, Mass., 1968, p. 43, and W. A. Lewis, *The Theory of Economic Growth*, London, 1956, p. 59.

the public with responsibility for implementation. But a considerable number of changes are necessary.

Specialists in development problems need appropriate training over and above that traditionally given graduate students in anthropology. A specialist must gain more than passing acquaintance with tropical agriculture, for instance, development economics, education theory, forestry, law, and public administration. After this, specialization in more depth can take place. The need is for social science research, though in view of personal inclination this will mean specialization in anthropology and *intimate* knowledge of the problems and techniques in other disciplines. And, if graduate students are to be trained then practical experience in a government setting would seem essential.

The theoretical problems are, to my mind, brutally simple, and brutally hard. These are: (1) how to operate effectively in multidisciplinary research given the tremendous expansion of knowledge and literature; (2) how to achieve some meaningful coincidence between the concerns of all social scientists so that those charged with decision-making are not presented with a baffling array of suggestions; (3) how to use anthropological literature so as to make statements of national import. The practical consideration is that a thorough assessment of the administrative scene must be made; when an accurate survey reveals what is known then research design can take place. At all costs one wants to avoid the academic revealing as 'an advance' something that the administrator has been well aware of for a long time.

Personally the academic is going to have to feel a commitment, or he is going to have to be fascinated by the problems. His academic experience will be more vital, more real, and more enjoyable than the old confused establishment line on community development. He will argue his case with policymakers but he will not, as he did so often in the past, simply assert that he is right without a careful review of *all* the facts. It is thoughts and observations like these which lead me to say that applied anthropology never had much to do with academic life.

The applied anthropologist was not a *representative* of academic anthropology in developing countries, he belonged in private *professional* practice.[6] The requirement to do something, to exercise power over events or people, and the characteristic ingredients of the decision-making process, opinion based on experience and knowledge, placed the applied anthropologist in the professional milieu of doctors and lawyers. This brings me to the second part of my argument against applied anthropology, the need for a general practitioner class.

Each year in universities all over the world thousands of men and women are trained in anthropology to M.A. standards. If they do not wish to remain in university life then virtually no avenues of employment are open to them which would utilize their special knowledge. As I have said, I feel sure that many would welcome an opportunity to undertake development work, and that this is a service which anthropology departments should have undertaken before now. There is something vaguely unrealistic and slightly selfish about an entirely academic anthropology though I do not deny the benefit to the wider world of those who embrace academia. But, then, anthropology is concerned with general intellectual development rather than the inculcation of professional skills.

What would be required to harness the talents of these trained people? For a start further training along the lines already suggested: that is, familarity with disciplines and professions that should cooperate on development work. Assuming the right temperament and academic performance I see the next step as an internship in a government or an international agency for one or two years. Successful completion of this should lead to certification. I can see a valuable and rewarding career for such people. I would envisage generalists at the M.A. level and specialist practitioners at the Ph.D. level. But, could jobs be provided?

It is difficult to overcome the past. If faculty show interest,

6. Both Goodenough, *Cooperation in Change*, New York 1963, and Foster, *Traditional Cultures: And the Impact of Technological Change*, New York, 1962, and *Applied Anthropology*, Boston, 1969, maintain that the applied anthropologist and the academic anthropologist are of the same genus though specialization may promote different species. I think they are the same species though of a different genus.

and then departments; if foundations can be persuaded to fund preliminary programs; if professional associations can make their concern known to governments and international agencies; if the interns perform well . . . I would be devastated by all the 'ifs' were it not for the fact that I believe that pressure from students of anthropology can bring these kinds of programs into being. Naturally there will be resistance from those faculty who are unwilling to learn new things and from those who have benefited from 'applied' work. But anthropology in North America and elsewhere could do with a little spring cleaning.

Academic anthropology has, for too long, been used as a home department for applied anthropologists. The academic anthropologist is interested in understanding the problems that the applied anthropologist has been interested in solving or influencing. Both will benefit to the extent that a clear demarcation is made between their respective roles and spheres of influence.

Why not an anthropology of development or *development anthropology* with a general practitioner class known as *development anthropologists?* If academic anthropologists call what they do development anthropology when it is involved with the kinds of social change associated with modernization or other situations where the people themselves express great unhappiness with their lot, or in interdisciplinary work connected with social or economic growth, they have not, through choice of an unfortunate name, made a commitment to predict or produce social change. They will study and analyze—scholarly functions. Their discipline will have come more into line with development administration and development economics. It is more likely to attract serious anthropologists than an applied science which is an ossified piece of anthropological history alive with moral worms.

I said that advisedly because the whole question of relativism, the equation of 'my' morality with 'his' is an impossible one to answer. Undoubtedly ethical questions and issues must be fully explored not with the aim of providing an intellectual tool kit of responses but with the hope that the individual's sensitivity toward problems will be increased. It is not really one's anthropological knowledge alone which can bring into focus the moral issues involved in development work. Taking decisions, reaching conclusions about right and wrong depends on one's personal history, experience, and kinds of intellectual training. Our aim must be educative in the first place, to try to let people have a wide enough range of facts to make a decision. We will not achieve good moral decision theory just as we have not developed infallible models in other areas of life. The gap between the ideal and the actual must be narrowed as much as is humanly possible.

There seem to me to have been three main philosophical streams or trends. The first derives a license to act in a cross-cultural setting from the proposition that peoples of all cultures dislike disease and pain, therefore action to alleviate is permissible. This is sound, though it is the extension of action in this sanctioned sphere to other areas of life that we must beware of. Second is the proposition that where people have requested change, action to secure this is permissible. Here it is necessary to ensure that one places all known knowledge of the possible consequences of change in the hands of the people, so that they can confirm their decision. Last is the rather tenuous proposition that those responsible for change believe it will be a 'good thing' for the people and even if they do not now clamor for such changes they will appreciate them in due course. This is a common idea because of the exigencies of time, the difficulty in educating everyone exposed to change, and the dictates of political authority. Pessimistically, I would say the last idea is the most common. Realistically, I would urge that anthropologists continue to educate themselves as to what this means in reality, and that they also try to educate planners more than they have done in the past. There will be shortfalls and unethical actions and plans. The question of whether to disassociate oneself from or to try to work within an organization to promote change is not for me to answer. But I can say the question will arise.

Dealing with moral issues, many applied anthropologists have adopted an analogy with the position of the physician. Mention is made of care, a duty to avoid harm to one's clients, the need to guard against negligence, and so on. These notions are a comment on the negative side of morality but they do not effectively deal with the positive side. They do not pay sufficient attention to what ought to be done, as opposed to what ought not to be done.

Statements bearing on the need for positive moral actions are usually derived from their correlate on the negative side. Duty to avoid harm becomes intention to abolish harm as far as is practical; lack of financial and intellectual resources is seen as a harm and is translated into a positive program to raise incomes and provide educational opportunities. A quite materialistic and Western picture emerges: 'progress' is moral, and where a recommendation to increase the quantity of money and various kinds of opportunity is thought commensurate with the discharge of one's ethical and moral responsibilities. Provided I do no harm and believe that my actions will do some good, then as far as the Society for Applied Anthropology is concerned I may meet my colleagues with an easy conscience.[7]

No one would deny the importance of an improvement in the material circumstances of the citizens of developing countries, but to whom, if not the anthropologist, are we to look for guidance on cultural matters affecting the quality of life?

The ethical code of the applied anthropologists [8] pays no attention to cultural issues in the layman's sense of the term. In fact, despite the lectures on values given to nonanthropologists, the application of this knowledge by anthropologists themselves has been predominantly limited to materialistic issues. In all applied anthropology, where is the recognition of moral and ethical responsibility toward the art, drama, music, and literature of 'clients,' the emphatic recognition that these are an intrinsic good in themselves and that anthropologists have a duty to pay attention not only to the material aspect of life but also to the quality of existence? Goodenough's sole advice to nonanthropologists on aesthetic forms of expression is instructive:

We know, of course, that recreational and religious institutions function in many more ways than helping people to handle their chronic frustrations or chronic anxieties stemming from childhood frustrations.

7. See Foster's discussion in *Applied Anthropology*, pp. 173-179.
8. *Human Organization*, XXII (963-64), p. 237.

But we need only think of the predominance given by Christian leaders to the problem of the "fleshy" desires to be reminded that those of our wants whose gratification is heavily curtailed or entirely disallowed by our public values and our rules of conduct remain a problem in our emotional or spiritual life. To make up for our inability to gratify these desires directly we have institutional ways of indulging them vicariously, as with our calendar and billboard art. And advertising regularly appeals to the young, middle class, American housewife, driven by the many needs of husband and children and without another adult woman in the house to share her responsibilities, by appealing to her frustrated desire for time to attend to her own wants with picture displays of her imagined self in attitudes of extreme languor and narcissistic self-indulgence. If we continue in this vein of thought, we may well begin to wonder how much of what we represent to ourselves and to others as the benefits of the American way of life are institutionalized fantasies we have created in order to indulge vicariously those of our desires that are chronically frustrated for most of us in real life. If such a thought repels us as heresy, we perceive thereby how important were the fantasies and dreams in which people indulge in more acceptable manner the wants that their daily responsibilities and duties within the social order do not permit them to gratify.

Occasional licensed indulgence of normally frustrated wants of their vicarious gratification in art, literature, mythology, drama and other forms of fantasy or play acting by no means complete the roster of techniques for dealing with the emotional problems frustration helps to generate—For us these psychoanalytic concepts are convenient points of departure from which to illustrate the complexities and subtleties of human values.[9]

If this is what aesthetic forms of expression can mean then I do not suppose any Peace Corps volunteer or applied anthropologist is to be blamed if he fails to preserve or improve these features. It would obviously be better to get at the real problems which of course the 'client' resists or is unaware of. It could turn into quite a benign form of cenorship always, of course, assuming that the 'operator' does not have problems of his own.

The war in Vietnam, the military-industrial complex, and the activities of the Central Intelligence Agency have become such

9. Goodenough, *Co-operation in Change*, pp. 118-119.

pressing concerns that anthropologists increasingly question the
feasibility of a posture of neutrality. I do not personally feel that
one can be neutral when confronted by these issues or by the
agonizing problems of developing countries. However, the existence of concern has not pointed to any particular role. I think
there is growing agreement that individual anthropologists
should adopt a stance with regard to public issues, and that in
teaching, in relations with authorities or the wider public they
should cogently reveal the logic and reasoning behind their personal opinions.

Berreman [10] has written a thoughtful and sensitive paper on
the social responsibilities of the anthropologist that illustrates
some quite common fallacies about the role of the 'intellectual.'

(a) Alfred Schutz suggested that "it is the duty and the privilege of
the well-informed citizen in a democratic society to make his private
opinion prevail over the public opinion of the man in the street." This
is not done by force but by reason.

If this is true the universities should control our lives. Why,
then, elections? The analogy with a judge and jury is useful.
Questions of law are to be determined by the judge, issues of
fact are for jury decision. I do not think the position of the social scientists should be any different. People who love, hope,
or fear, and who cannot rival the social scientist in reasoned
argument are not to be disenfranchised. And, as Kierkegaard
said: "Life can only be understood backwards but it must be
lived forwards." Schutz's conception of the intellectuals' duty
is understandable, but the resultant opinions ought not, and
will not, always prevail simply through force of reason. Reason
always must depend on values, and for this reason, many notions about the role of the academic appear unduly ethnocentric.
After all what is the role of reason in the Arab-Israeli conflict?

(b) Either the social sciences know more than do *de facto* leaders of the
culture as to what the findings of research mean, as to the options the institutional system presents, as to what human personalities want, why they

10. G. D. Berreman, "Is Anthropology Alive? Social Responsibility in Social
Anthropology," *Current Anthropology*, December 1968.

want them, and how desirable changes can be affected, *or* the vast current industry of social science is an empty façade.[11]

This statement is quite true as it stands, and I do not doubt the knowledge of the social sciences. But I have never met and had the advice of the social sciences and seriously doubt if I ever shall. What I have met is the *individual* social scientist whose grasp of what has been done is really only a fragmentary representation of that 'vast current industry.' A collection of individuals present similar problems, because their opinions do not coalesce sufficiently.

As far as the anthropologist goes it has not been my intention to deny his potential utility; rather my concern has been to show that unless he informs himself more adequately on what could be done and how, his observations are only likely to attract the interest and attention of his academic colleagues. And, if anthropologists do possess unique ability to carry out successful social engineering, I must confess myself bemused by the quirk of fate which has enabled *nonintellectuals* to organize and run quite large institutional endeavors in a manner that compares quite favorably with university departments.

We need to attract the best scholars to work on problems of modernization, urbanization, or even of standardization in the social sciences. We cannot continue the present trend of dabbling in applied anthropology by eminent scholars. Scholars seem to feel that they can only indulge in applied work if they have made a significant contribution in the general field of anthropology. Problems in development work can only be tackled on a full-time basis. These scholars can train graduate students who wish to have professional careers as general practitioners and also those who wish to teach. Unless anthropologists themselves take the initiative and demonstrate how vital a contribution their subject can make, things are going to remain as they are.

It required a horrendous lack of imagination to keep trotting out the applied anthropologist's prayer, repeated in many introductory texts: "I believe in the Golden stool episode, the Vicos

11. Lynch quoted in Berreman, *ibid.*

episode, the universal value and crucial importance of community development, and in the miraculous efficacy of 'cultural principles' in development work." Malicious? Yes! Deniable? No!

IV

Tension in the Field

Why is it that relationships between administrators and anthropologists in the field are often strained? It is not disciplines or professions that clash but attitudes. I have had administrative experience in the southwest Pacific, and I would like to show typical administrative attitudes in relation to anthropologists and their work. The continued existence of poor or strained relationships is neither good anthropology nor sound administrative practice. In this case it was the Pacific Islanders who suffered when relationships in the fields were bad.

Relationships in the Solomon Islands were fairly cordial until Marching Rule—(see my *Big Men and Cargo Cults*, 1970) though there were occasional personality clashes. Government in the Solomons, until after World War II, did little more than keep the peace. During this period missionaries and commercial expatriates seem to have attracted the majority of anthropological criticism. The Solomons became a major theater in the Pacific war. Missions, governments, and planters suffered heavy losses. Administrative officers left the territory to join up and those who had remained were badly in need of leave. It was a time of extreme crisis for the administration.[1] Peace brought little relief.

1. Western Pacific High Commission press release, Public Relations Office, Suva 31 July 1948; *Among Those Present*, Central Office of Information, London, 1966 ed.

This was the time when Marching Rule began. There was a shortage of funds and experienced staff. However, the Protectorate began, in the late 1940's, to receive administrative replacements. Many of these cadet administrative officers had only recently come out of the armed services and had no previous civil service experience. Then, during this crucial period, anthropologists began to offer serious criticisms of government policy.

C. S. Belshaw's *Island Administration in the South West Pacific* (1950) attracted the attention of government officers. Belshaw had been an administrative cadet in the Solomons. The Western Pacific High Commission has never been able to work out to its own satisfaction how any cadet could have anything authoritative, or even useful, to say about administration. Traditionally cadets had been the lowest form of administration life, and a number of senior officers did not take kindly to the advice given in the book. The government reaction was unduly sensitive. But the initial irritation was sustained by a growing realization that anthropologists had begun to regard themselves as guardians of "their people."

Then came a more serious blow, Peter Worsley's *The Trumpet Shall Sound* (1957). Worsley had never been in the Solomons though he severely criticized the administration. He had limited access to government records and really nothing other than a good degree of intuition on which to base his very strongly worded criticisms of government policy. Senior government officers in Honiara, the postwar capital of the Solomons, were not slow to appreciate that there was much in these books that had nothing to do with the kind of anthropology that they had known in prewar days. Government began to sheer away from contact with anthropology. Many government officers began to feel, and have felt ever since, that to have an anthropologist around was not much different from having a reporter from a sensationalist newspaper in the area. Though the tradition of island hospitality tended to obscure tensions—attitudes have hardened on both sides.

In the absence of an informed local press the administration was unaccustomed to criticism of government policy and, instead of recognizing the legitimate function of such comment, officers tended to regard those who protested as troublemakers. The trouble was that anthropologists were virtually the only people who offered criticism of government action. Things have changed but the anthropological image lingers.

Anthropologists would never have talked about Pacific islanders in the same way that they referred to the government and its policies. They believed that their work began and ended with the Pacific islander. Anthropologists continue to show a curious inability to admit, even to themselves, that their dislike of government officers is often the product of a personal political view and emotional bias rather than scientific training. A criticism that can be leveled at the kinds of things that anthropologists have written about colonialism in the Pacific is that much of it is simply bad anthropology. Is it anthropology at all?

Anthropologists often arrived in the field having read all the pertinent data on their area but not having done any 'homework' on the administration itself. I have frequently, during my government service, been irritated by anthropologists who, though they are acquainted with all the published anthropological literature, make snap judgments about government without any attempt to read the documents setting out government policy. Many anthropologists almost wholly utilitized time in the capital or at a district H.Q. seeking out informants from their area—very few took the opportunity to ask serious questions about government policy or even how the system of government functioned. Government officers complain among themselves that anthropologists who have wholly confined their research to an isolated community often are unqualified in terms of such experience to make statements about the nature of government policy for the whole territory. It is hard to see how anthropologists can claim area specialization when they have made little or no attempt to visit other regions.

Administrators usually feel responsible for the safety and well being of anthropologists in their areas. Is the anthropologist's wife all right, have they enough to eat, when were they last heard from, why have they not come upon the radio, has there been an "anthropogrom," could she have been raped while while he was away in the bush? Most administrators entertain such thoughts at one time or another; they are alleviated when a well equipped man or sound husband and wife team arrive who obviously have everything worked out; they are aggravated when anthropologists have plainly not thought out the matter of how they are going to live, how they are going to obtain housing and supplies. Added to these worries, some of which administrators admittedly tend to create for themselves, is the regrettable fact that some universities send people who are emotionally unsuited to spending long periods on their own. When administrative services are taken for granted, and when an anthropologist, who has not discussed or even indicated his personal dissatisfaction with government policy, returns home to write a critical account of the administration, a very sour taste is left.

Few anthropologists take the trouble to hide their feeling that the expatriates have never had it so good. Expatriates are less than happy with this posture. They point out that the anthropologists have not themselves arrived to do anything for the people and that they use Pacific islanders as much as possible to advance their personal careers. When anthropologists pick a fieldwork area, administrators ask, do they tend to wonder, not what they can do for thepeople, but what the people can do for them? Undeniably there are, and have been, poor administrators but it would also be true to say that some anthropologists did not appear to administrators to be eminently suited to their profession either. It is fundamental, both for good fieldwork and good administration, to be able to operate officially or professionally in such a way that the effects of personal bias are eliminated. There have been mistakes on both sides.

The giving of gratuitous advice to administrations in the preface to scholarly works, or in the text, is often irritating for a number of quite sound reasons. Anthropologists, if they wish to continue to offer suggestions about what governments should do, or how they should do what they are doing, would need to make their advice very much more specific and idiomatic. They would have to pay more attention than they have done to date to the fact that what is good for their region or small community may be bitterly opposed by people of another region or island.

Seen from the standpoint of all the inhabitants of a particular territory there is really—as I have said—no such thing as an optimal policy in any sphere of administrative activity. Anthropologists cannot imply as they often do when they pass value judgments on government policy that they have some value system which enables them to decide what ought to be done. No matter what an administration does—or even a government in a metropolitan country—there will undoubtedly be some degree of public disagreement.

We have judgments of government activity without fact collection or fieldwork, which yield opinions divested of science. Neither individually nor collectively, in the form of professional associations, have anthropologists shown that they have anything really useful to say about the problems of the Pacific Islands as a whole, as opposed to the future of their community. It is quite easy and fashionable to criticize the various administrations, but what is to replace them?

If the anthropologists wish to voice political opinions or personal bias against colonialism in the Pacific a logical step would be to take demonstrative action in the home country since those abroad work for London, Canberra, Paris, and Washington. This has not happened on any sizable scale. The administrator in the Pacific ought not to be, as he is at present, the *sole* recipient of criticism. Administrators who read anthropologists' criticisms of Australian policy in New Guinea, for example, wonder privately among themselves why certain territories should continually be singled out for criticism while others, notably West Irian, the French and the United States trust territories, escape serious comment and evaluation.

Anthropologists often receive ethnographic data from expatriates. While many of the observations that these expatriates make are inaccurate or not justifiable in terms of the empirical data, undoubtedly a number of valuable pointers for research are given. Typically, the nature of the anthropologists 'thank you' is to make some brief mention in the preface of his book or article, which implies that the expatriate was helpful, gave him tea, carried his bags, helped him relax from intellectual toil. We should really see far more acknowledgment of ideas and pieces of information than is the case at present. Anthropologists are fairly widely accused of plagiarizing the ideas of administrators, technical officers, missionaries, and planters.

The record of administrative usage of anthropological advice is not an enlightened one, and much of the anthropological comment on administrators and their policies has not been in the best traditions of their discipline. Neither administration nor anthropology nor those we would seek to aid are helped by a coolness between anthropology and administration.

V

Misunderstanding Community Development

There is a growing tendency, especially among anthropologists [1] to assume that any aid process which affects a community can be thought of as a form of community development. Existing literature on community development deals with the 'nuts and bolts': how to build, what spray to use to avoid malaria, whether to dig or construct. However, insufficient attention has been paid to implications stemming from the adoption of new methods in community development work. Simply in terms of strategy I want to examine the advantages of the traditional approach to community development [2] over some current methods which involve trained personnel, large capital outlay, and a be-

1. W. H. Goodenough, *Cooperation in Change,* New York, 1963, pp. 15–30; C. J. Erasmus, *Man Takes Control,* Minneapolis, 1961, pp. 320–323; G. M. Foster, *Traditional Cultures: And the Impact of Technological Change,* New York, 1962, pp. 183–186.
2. I rely here on personal experience of community development in the Pacific. My intention is to concentrate on the principles involved in community development rather than to identify specific agencies or their officers (who in most cases are not able to defend themselves). I am solely responsible for the opinions and statements expressed here and any errors that it may contain. It does not necessarily reflect the opinions of the Western Pacific High Commission or its officers.

lief that results can form a development blueprint.[3] I want to
suggest that community development projects are of limited
value anyway since the major impetus for development must
come from government extension services. Many programs have
been virtually divorced from the recipient government's extension services.[4] The boundary between community and other
forms of development has become blurred. Existing approaches
to community development are often poorly coordinated and expensive in terms of what they actually achieve.[5] In the new development philosophies the principles of self-help and choice
have become of secondary importance. Emphasis has now been
placed on the prediction and production of social change.

Community development used to be thought of as self-help.
The idea gained popularity in situations where a government
could not answer needs or demands within its existing extension
services. This kind of development was self-sustaining and relatively autonomous. It was also directly related to the needs, capacities, and specialties of the community.[6] Envisaged was a
kind of growth which would not require a great deal of financial
assistance, technical expertise, or lengthy involvement of valuable personnel. The major effort had to come from the people
themselves.

In some situations community development has been offered
by a government as a kind of first aid.[7] Backward or remote
areas which have been impervious to normal extension methods
have been involved in community development projects in an
attempt to get members of these communities to the stage where
they can participate in normal extension services. Alternatively,

3. R. N. Adams *et al.*, *Social Change in Latin America Today*, New York,
1960.
4. H. S. Adams, G. M. Foster, & P. S. Taylor, *Report on Community Development Programs in India, Pakistan, and the Philippines,* Washington,
D.C., 1955; W.C. Gibson, H. S. Masters, E. F. Wittee, *Report on Community Development Programs in India, Iran, Egypt, and the Gold Coast,*
Washington, D.C., 1955.
5. Erasmus, *Man Takes Control.*
6. See T. R. Batten, *Communities and Their Development,* London, 1957,
for a common sense treatment of community development.
7. D. G. Cochrane, "The Administration of Wagina Resettlement Scheme,"
Human Organization, Summer 1970.

community development has been used in a once-and-for-all technical innovation or construction project which has been requested by the people themselves. Traditionally, community development has been an abnormal method, as opposed to normal, and it has focused on a community, as opposed to the wider application of normal extension services.[8]

Community development meant development of human potential through self-education. Concerned with helping people to define or appreciate their wants and letting them evolve the means of their satisfaction, it attempted to involve the whole community. Schemes concentrated on existing thoughts and aspirations rather than simply becoming administrative in seeking to implement preconceived plans. Creation came from within the community rather than from without. To stimulate this process a member of the community was often given specialist training, or an alien development agent was added to the community at the request of the people themselves.

There is a tremendous difference between *affecting* a community through preconceived or expert-led commercial construction, health, or educational programs, and *developing* a community so that the people themselves are in control of the innovating impetus. The first approach is properly part of a normal government extension program. The second approach is where the community becomes a repository for inspiration, technical know-how, and progress, i.e., community development.

Centrally conceived schemes with an elaborate administrative hierarchy reaching out of the community to a capital or some aid-giving agency's regional center are not community development.[9] Schemes which have preset targets, and which incidentally try to involve members of a community, are a function of normal government extension work, or they are something that

8. This has been the case in the Pacific Island territories. From conversations with senior administrators from Africa and Asia (attending the Oxford University courses in Government and Development in 1964–65 and 1967–68), I have concluded that this was the general philosophy elsewhere.

9. H. S. Adams, *et al., Programs in India, Pakistan, and the Philippines;* Gibson, *et al., Programs in India, Iran, Egypt, and the Gold Coast;* Erasmus, *Man Takes Control,* pp. 163–164, provide examples.

has been delegated to an alien aid-giving agency—they are also not community development.

Community development is pretty much of a trial balloon. It should be incompatible with rigid targets, objectives, or presentation of plans to the community on a take-it-or-leave-it basis. Consequently a distinction can and should be made between government extension workers and the role of a development agent in a community. Development agents are not normally the equivalent of civil servants. They ought to be people not so very much more knowledgeable or competent than members of the community they serve. People are needed as development agents who are fallible, human, convinced that they are jumping off the deep end, and, hopefully, lacking in ideological commitment and missionary zeal.

The development agent becomes a prominent citizen in a community. He should concentrate on the development of that community and not simply on a single facet of its social life, i.e., wells or new plant types. Development agents should not think of themselves as 'technicians' or 'operators'; [10] they must think of themselves as human beings first, and as citizens of their community. The development agent is not the bearer of Western know-how confronting a backward and unfortunate community. And he is not to subtly subvert the people's customs in an effort to mold the community to his own image of modernity. Development agents can only properly work in such a way that the impetus for change comes from the people themselves—as I said earlier, the service they perform for the community should be that of the midwife and not that of the surgeon. People in a community must be allowed to do what they want. By directing, organizing, and executing their own projects they demonstrate the kind of development that they want to participate in. At the community level scientific knowledge is no substitute for human warmth, tact, sympathy, and understanding. A development agent who demonstrates these qualities can afford to make mistakes, and he will be forgiven. Few communities really expect strangers to know their language, customs, and history. When

10. Goodenough, *Cooperation in Change*, uses these terms.

the development agent and community members both proceed from a position of mutual ignorance, the learning process strengthens ties of friendship. And most primitive communities like to give just as much as they like to receive.

Community development ought not to involve any assumption that people can be manipulated. Even those who believe in the insidious suggestion that development agents should attempt to innovate by changing the customs of the community where they are guests [11] should carefully examine their mandate to change a people's culture. People in a community may want change but they will inevitably wish to enjoy such change within the rhythm and the framework of their own traditional society.[12] This is a point which economists sometimes overlook.[13]

The backward community has been a blindspot for governments in many developing countries. In post World War II days few administrators minded if communities were inspired to cooperative ventures in trading, water conservation, and hygiene. Objectives of community development were small scale and had few implications for national development. It did not appear that there was much to be gained from teaching things such as home economics. Few of the projects could be expanded. Innovation did not seem to spread from community to community. When the West declared a war on want, the community became a fulcrum for much of the aid-giving process. The community was a fairly neutral area, and this kind of development had the advantage of avoiding confrontation with the host government.

Westerners started with a desire to do something. Men, money, and machines poured into the developing countries. Unfortunately a large slice of this aid went to community development, and insufficient attention was paid to improving the extension services of the recipient government. Gradually the

11. C. M. Arensberg and A. H. Niehoff, *Introducing Social Change*, Chicago, 1964, p. 9; E. H. Spicer (ed.), *Human Problems in Technological Change*, New York, 1965, p. 13; Goodenough, *Cooperation in Change*, pp. 346–347.
12. R. Thurnwald, "Price of the White Man's Peace," *Pacific Affairs*, IX, no. 3.
13. D. G. Cochrane, Review of J. S. G. Wilson's *Economic Survey of the New Hebrides*, *Economica*, May, 1968.

original function of community development changed as the American philosophy of community development [14] became more popular.

Development agents were trained to accomplish objectives. Instead of being self-sufficient, projects had extensive financial support. In place of community autonomy and evolvement, central planning and an administrative hierarchy linked the development agent with the donor nation. Then the universities moved in and academics began to create a new sub-discipline out of community development. As the Western nations' colonial services disbanded, little attempt was made to tap the experience which colonial civil servants had built up through the years. Instead, these lessons are now being relearned—it seems an incredibly wasteful process. Arensberg and Niehoff, Foster, and Goodenough (see bibliography) encourage development agents to produce change, and at the same time they stress that community development has become more scientific as a result of anthropological involvement.

Much of what I have read about the new scientific community development is common knowledge among all levels of government personnel in the field. *Unfortunately many administrators have never set down their experience of community development.* Foster has rightly said: "There is very little mechanism to make available to new personnel the accumulated wisdom of earlier programs." [15] The mechanism could, in fact, exist. There are many senior and experienced retired administrators who have not been consulted—surely it would pay to take a representative sample of their views?

International agencies and affluent nations concentrated on showcase community development in a manner which not only was intended to help the recipient community but which also served to demonstrate to the host country how it should tackle development. Community development became a means rather than an end in itself. Many governments now feel obliged, because of the status of the donor, to accept showcase schemes de-

---

14. Foster, *Traditional Cultures*, pp. 183–186.
15. *Traditional Cultures*, p. 239.

signed in regional centers which, while they may look good on paper, were not drawn up with the specific needs of an individual country in mind.[16]

There is something unpleasant about community development philosophies which talk of 'resistance'[17] or the 'utilization of existing institutions' in such a way that the suspicions of the recipient community will not be aroused.[18]

Many of these schemes harass people. Communities are exhorted, lectured to, and so on. Poor people all over the world confronting reforming zeal would probably rather be left alone. The developing countries should not have to provide a clinic for nations who need to prove how kind and generous they are or a brave new world for their nationals who cannot stand home. Development agents should be engaged on the assumption that they are going to do a job for which they will receive payment in terms of salary and experience. The present Peace Corps (the equivalent of Volunteer Service Overseas of Britain) practice of paying a pittance gives assignments a missionary aura and encourages the idea possessed by many idealistic volunteers that they are waging a crusade on disease, poverty, and ignorance. Volunteers should be paid what they are worth.

A great deal of money has been spent. Many people have been harassed. Are the results any better than those which could have been achieved if the funds had been given directly to the governments concerned? (Corruption in the local civil service is no argument against this. The way to combat corruption is to improve the local civil service not avoid it.) In a showcase scheme to improve water supplies, a soil scientist, a geologist, a public health expert, an engineer, and an anthropologist may be required.[19] The execution of these projects is often logical in

16. See Erasmus, *Man Takes Control*, p. 164. In the Solomons the same kind of thing has happened with W.H.O. sponsored improved village water supply schemes, and U.N.E.S.C.O. projects for the teaching of English as a second language.

17. Gouldner in A. W. Gouldner and S. M. Miller (eds.), *Applied Sociology*, New York 1965, pp. 5–21.

18. D. Lerner and W. Schramm, *Communications and Change in the Developing Countries*, Honolulu, 1967.

19. Erasmus, *Man Takes Control*, mentions this problem on p. 179.

Western terms but inappropriate in local circumstances. To afford expert-led community development, a nation first needs a well-developed economy.

What can we reasonably expect from community development? It cannot be thought of as a sound basis for national planning since each community is a unique collection of individuals who will not, no matter how many plans are drawn up, respond uniformly to the same suggestion. Current strategy is beginning to increase the cost of community development but it is not noticeably increasing its effectiveness because people are not really learning to help themselves. Communities depend on unearned money and outside expertise, and this cannot help the development of self-reliance and the knowledge that members of the community have the ability to change their circumstances. Erasmus[20] is highly critical of the self-help idea in community development, and he refers to people being expected to lift themselves up by their bootstraps. He commits, I think, the error of confusing community development with development initiated and sustained by a government's extension services. It is at the government extension service level that people cannot be expected to help themselves without substantial aid.

Many development agents are now taught to believe that they should innovate. Most are not highly trained in any discipline and have little experience of development work. They are unaware of the harmful effects that may be brought about by changing people's customs deliberately. Development agents have one or two years—sometimes even less—to produce results. Their superiors need results in order to justify expenditure of vast sums of public money. A response must come from the community whether the people are willing or not. If the people resist then the advice of the anthropologists can be brought into play by development agents. This kind of approach does not always arise from a disinterested concern to help but more often from a desire to make people conform to the Western development model—"the only logical model for development"[21]—and to show how useful our own development philosophies are.

20. *Ibid.*
21. Lerner and Schramm, *Communications*, p. 310.

There is a danger of arrogance in a form of reasoning, surely, where social scientists see culture as an irrational impediment to progress. Daniel Lerner says "I am persuaded that . . . Asian ethnocentrism is not merely a self indulgent nuisance but actually a major obstacle to development progress."[22] Fortunately the anthropological view is more fair, even if many applied texts appear to be saying much the same kind of thing.

Development agents at the community level are now being encouraged to sell their wares like salesmen. And, like salesmen, they are also taught how to make people buy things which they do not really want. Some anthropologists have even equated the goals of an American businessman and a development agent.[23]

In the midst of rather dubious empire building by academics, the young Western volunteer development agents are the sole ray of hope. If they are not too trained and prepared they can succeed in accomplishing many of the traditional objectives in community development. Volunteers will probably gain more, in the form of experience, than the community does in terms of development. We must not lose sight of the fact that one of the major functions of these volunteer schemes is to give the development agent himself a valuable form of training and experience. In this way the donor country benefits through the development of its volunteers. This must be stressed in the recipient country so that the relationship between agent and his community can be put on a businesslike footing. Developing communities, like other communities, are suspicious of idealists who offer something for nothing. Development agents should be made aware of the need to let the people in their community 'do their own thing.' The volunteers cannot be regarded as a major force for change in the developing countries.

Community development is not the place for the expert or for massive financial assistance. It should be thought of as an abnormal and unusual form of development. Expert-led-and-executed showcase schemes which have usually only minimally involved local people neither develop a community in its best

22. *Ibid.*, p. 110.
23. Arensberg and Niehoff, *Social Change*, p. 1.

interests nor do they provide a blueprint for broader application. It is necessary to concentrate on ideas of self-help and utilization of existing resources by avoiding as far as possible capital outlay and through provision of development agents who will not attempt to lead and direct community schemes in an effort to achieve predetermined results. As far as aid donors are concerned, the main development impetus should be phrased within the recipient governments' extension services.

Young volunteers can perform a valuable service both for themselves and for the community they serve. They should be under the administrative control of the recipient government. Development agents should be made to understand that they are not expected to change people's customs. If strategy in community development became traditional again it would yield a genuine form of development because it would make clear the distinction between imposition from without and evolvement from within the community.

Undoubtedly, there are a number of common sense rules about community development which can profitably be set down on paper so that development agents can learn something before going to the field. However, in the main, this kind of development requires personal qualities which cannot be taught anymore than we can teach a man to be a good administrator. There is no substitute for personal experience. Even if a man has mastered the relevant literature this is no guarantee that he will be effective at the community level.

Logically the people who should teach community development are those who have successfully executed a series of schemes. Anthropologists (Arensberg and Niehoff, Goodenough, etc.) are now putting forward guidelines abstracted from the study of community development projects all over the world, and, at the same time, they stress the utility of grasping cultural principles. This approach is self-defeating since each community, which is unique, is itself part of a unique culture. Development agents usually do not have the training or knowledge to be able to adjust these theoretical abstractions to local circumstances. And the anthropologists have not had sufficient practical experience to place their own contributions in perspective.

Foster has said: "In my experience the biggest blind spot of administrators is inability to understand the principle of scientific capital, the accumulation of theory and fact, general and specific, that has been built up painstakingly over a period of many years." [24] I suggest that in relation to community development the boot (or bootstrap to paraphrase Erasmus) is on the other foot.

24. *Traditional Cultures*, p. 248.

VI

Extension Work

In this chapter I want to put down the principles of extension work which are fairly common knowledge among technical officers, to highlight my contention that much of the applied anthropological advice has been a case of 'carrying coals to Newcastle.' Then I want to indicate where anthropology could be of service to extension workers.

As I remarked earlier it is important to distinguish community development from normal extension work. Development work in rural areas can be categorized as a series of activities concerned with extension or control. Controlling departments are responsible for provision of financial services, the maintenance of law and order, physical plant supervision, and so on. Extension departments are responsible for the implementation of a specific field program seeking to involve local people in say, medical matters, a preventive health routine, or with an agricultural program such as the planting and harvesting of new cash crops.

A program of extension activities involves specialist personnel who must try as far as possible to work together. This team should meet frequently. Each member explains his departmental policy, answers questions, seeks assistance, and agrees on his role in the over-all development pattern. At this point priorities can be agreed on, resources allocated, and the kinds of help that various departmental members can give and expect can be made clear to all who are involved in the extension program.

An action program in a rural area spanning several specialist fields must close ranks; it cannot afford to project a compartmentalized image. Villagers are unaware which specialist is responsible for what section or aspect of a program and may well ask the first extension worker who visits questions which are outside his field, though within the specialist sphere of one of his colleagues. To counter this possibility each member must arm himself with basic knowledge about all fields in the action program sufficient to be able to answer questions and to 'hold the line' until the real specialist is at hand. He must also be mindful of his other colleagues' interests even if he is not asked questions.

At the village level there could be nothing more dangerous than overdeveloped specialization; and the enthusiasm of people cannot be retained or their comprehension of what is going on improved if a specialist answers their questions by saying that he knows nothing, that they must wait until the specialist who does know visits.

Team members need the kind of training I term 'nonspecialized specialization.' That is, a person has specialized knowledge of one field, which is complemented by familiarity with or nonspecialized knowledge of other fields. Successful extension work is not a paper exercise; it relies on personal contact between specialists and villagers. The greater the contact, the more intimate its nature and the greater the chance of success. Exercise of specialist skill or leadership qualities either by professional or locally trained people must not be allowed—as has been the case in the West—to divorce the practitioner in his nonprofessional field from those he seeks to serve.

It is not an engineer's job just to build bridges, nor is it an educational expert's job just to examine schools. They can utilize their effectiveness in their own field at the same time they perform tasks for their colleagues. There is really no such thing as being 'off duty' in a good extension program.

We cannot afford to divorce leader from led; we cannot afford to marry to the technical and professional hierarchy a social hierarchy. We should not forget that the expertise of each professional in his specialist sphere is purchased at the cost of other talents. We must attempt to use the whole man as much as possible. The Western model does not. It is incredibly wasteful.

Too often Western job classifications and descriptions have been applied *mutatis mutandis* with little thought as to what is really required. Specialization should evolve from within a country rather than be imposed from without. Flexibility is the keynote and this is why I stress my concept of nonspecialized specialization. How does this actually work?

An extension worker adopts a counselor role in a noncoercive environment. Emphasis on personal neutrality by the specialist in the initial stages focuses everyone's attention on the issues at hand. Honesty and complete frankness are the only successful methods. If too grim a picture is painted then enthusiasm may be muted. If too rosy a picture is painted then when difficulties are encountered, confidence in the specialist will be imperiled.

If people decide to accept the advice of the extension worker then he can adopt a more positive role. He can begin to push measures to make the program take shape. However, in spite of this it must be made clear that responsibility for successful completion of the project rests with the people. The specialist will offer advice, criticism, or encouragement, as the case may be. Working up a good extension program requires thorough preparation.

Companies can assess their performance by reference to sales; but, governments cannot do this nor can extension teams. They must concentrate on obtaining as much 'feed back' as possible. An extension worker tries to build up an information network. He has informants who give a general account of what goes on; he has informants who can be relied on to put forward the action program's points in his village. And, of course, there is always an attempt to include men of influence in the network. Recruitment and maintenance of an informational network is the individual responsibility of each specialist as is evaluation of the material that these men provide.

The objectivity and authenticity of each piece of information is usually examined fairly closely in the early stages of a program. Has the news been confirmed by an independent source? Is it of village or regional significance? What degree of bias is there? What is the man's reason for giving the information? Building up this kind of network takes time, patience, hard work, and good judgment. However, although the kinds of information which come out are invaluable, the service is personal and the progenitor of a network cannot be sure that his successor can achieve the same degree of compatibility with his informants. This is why continuity of staff is very important in an extension program.

A new specialist must build up status. He must be accepted by the people as a friend before he can attempt to do extension work. A dynamic approach is usually out of place and confusing to people. One cannot experiment. Multiple changes cause disorientation and may create a crisis of confidence about the role of the individual extension worker. Theorizing—the search for neat solutions which will solve all problems—has unfortunately obscured the importance of the personal element in extension work.

'Institution building,' much favored by political scientists—it is unfortunate that they have not in the past felt it necessary to do fieldwork—has an appealing aura of persuasiveness and concreteness. The idea is not new. It was not discovered by social scientists but brought into being by colonial administrators in West Africa.[1] Institutions tend to be rigid and not always adaptable to new needs, ideas, and functions. Not very adaptable, that is, to social change. As constituents of systems of action they are concerned with behavioral norms, and as constituents of systems of belief they are concerned with values. They give rise to institutionalized patterns of behavior.

Social scientists are, in any developing country, concerned with change. Some talk of 'strategy' or of circumventing the unknown through the building of institutions.[2] We are often led by such people to believe that in this way we can indeed, in a

1. Sir Andrew Cohen, *British Policy in Changing Africa*, Evanston, 1959.
2. D. Lerner and W. Schramm, *Communications and Change in the Developing Countries*, Honolulu, 1967. See also W. B. Hamilton (ed.), *The Transfer of Institutions*, Durham, North Carolina, 1964.

modest way, predict and produce social change. However, institution building must cover a vast number of organizational types and organizational purposes. Though seldom appreciated, the dangers of institutional specialization are also very great. The remarks I made about Western job classifications and descriptions can also apply to institutions.

We need in this sphere to have nonspecialized institutions capable of performing multiple functions. Values and beliefs may change quickly even in spite of the existence of a vigorous extension program, and the last thing that is required is to build the kinds of institutions which are incapable of accommodating a wide variety of changes and responses. The 'new institutions' may themselves, in a short period of time, become obstacles to progress.

For example, instead of having a rural post office we could have something that could do postal work, disseminate information on agriculture, and give medical advice; instead of a young farmers' club we could have an institution which is a focusing point for complete action programs and not just for the single facet, agriculture, as is so often the case at present. The advantage of this kind of approach is that it preserves organizational skills without dissipating them over a wide compartmentalized area; it safeguards leadership skills which may well be in short supply; it gives rise to a multi-purpose organizational framework which may well be more successful in achieving goals because it accords with traditional kinds of organizational experience. The tragedy of many countries has been not so much the importation of inappropriate beliefs and kinds of knowledge as the creation of inappropriate institutions.

I need not say any more on institution building since I have made clear my belief that the essential nonspecialized role of the individual should also have its counterpart in the institutional sphere. Just as I remarked earlier that the possible atrophy of some of the talents of an expert was a feature I was concerned with highlighting, so too with institutions. Many institutions have unused resources and capabilities which are not utilized through conventional seeking of institutional goals. Hospitals can teach, agricultural stations can cure. And leadership is the same wherever it is seen, needed, and recognized. Western experience has been to decrease the amount of specialization the higher one goes in the social, economic, and political hierarchy.

Here it is suggested that this specialization ought to be totally reversed in the developing nations. Whereas economists, following the long tradition beginning with Adam Smith, believe that it is very important, and very good, to have a wide ranging division of labor,[3] I am saying that this is very dangerous and probably a bad thing, for most developing countries. I think our own experience has definitely led us astray here. Development concepts should surely be thematic rather than purely structural.

The Western model of development may be very out of place in the rural areas. We pay a price for specialization that we cannot afford; the truth of this is the evidence that we have failed in the developing countries to achieve the kind of progress that we must make in the agricultural sector. My suggestion—and I do not go any deeper into the matter here—is that we examine more closely the concept of nonspecialized specialization. On management grounds specialization should be delayed as long as possible.

A final word on communications, a new industry whose praises have been sung loud in the development literature, again by social scientists with little practical experience. Too loud. People still should be able to choose or reject advice; they should have the right to turn off the message or to ask that it be changed. This is one reservation. Another relates to the danger of the conversion of communications media for propaganda purposes. Another relates to the ability of the media pushers to stimulate demand out of proportion to ability to supply that demand. Mass media are effective when used in conjunction with good extension programs. But they are a *supplement.* Media

3. H. Liebenstein, *Economic Theory and Organizational Analysis,* New York, 1960, says that economists have not paid a great deal of attention to this issue. Durkheim's work on the division of labor—his ideas of mechanical and organic solidarity—was sociological. I am concerned with the implication for *management,* the free flow of information, ideas, technology, and the maximization of individual talent.

must be used in situations where there is also personal contact and 'feedback,' otherwise the pace of development may well become uneven.

Information services must have the advice of local people— perhaps anthropologists as well—in addition to the specialists. There must be a blend of the practical with the idiomatic; life must be made more than a grim march toward 'civilization,' with people being exhorted, lectured at, and compared. When people become too bothered, the important message is lost.

The language is appealing and persuasive. The idea that one should have a 'communications strategy,' and that one could think of the messages being subject to the so-called multiplier effect of the economist sounds marvelous.[4] But extension workers that I have talked to at the village level are not very impressed by the idea nor are social scientists who do fieldwork. That we should *communicate* is not very original and is a problem for technicians. *What* we should communicate is an entirely different matter which calls for the kinds of knowledge which an anthropologist or an experienced extension worker often possess. But no amount of 'new frontier' imagery should be permitted to persuade academics, and administrators who have not done extension work, that people can and will put up with being *manipulated.* The quick revolutionary breakthroughs that are heralded in development thinking from time to time must not obscure the fact that the real test takes place at the village level. Good extension work is really the key to development. With this a great number of things can happen; without it, most of what social scientists do is simply a paper game.

The trouble with social science proposals is often that they are incapable of being realized. The tendency to be logical and academic is indulged at the expense of appreciating the realities of the situation. If a fraction of what has been written had been translated into practice, the problems of developing countries would have long since vanished. This is why social scientists must take into account the knowledge and experience of men in

4. Lerner and Schramm, *Communications.* See also W. L. Schramm *The Process and Effects of Mass Communication,* Urbana, Illinois, 1965, and L. W. Doob, *Communication in Africa,* New Haven, 1961.

the field. They have a feel for what can be done. It is better to plan on the experience people have already gained, subsequently, injecting the fruits of academic experience, than to start with academic logic. I cannot sufficiently stress that planning is not to be divorced from real life experience. In the absence of sophisticated knowledge about change processes very careful attention has to be paid to the actual or potential contribution of extension workers.

Extension work is important for anthropologists, economists, and planners generally. That this is so and that is has not been adequately emphasized is an indication of how few social scientists have had practical experience of good extension work. For anthropologists it should be clear that good extension work does not raise moral problems: is not involved with the manipulation of people and the hard sell. The best kind of extension work is a process that most anthropologists should not be too troubled to participate in.

What, then, is the position of anthropology? What role could a development anthropologist play in extension work? To answer this it is necessary to return to the categories used in my general critique of applied anthropology, the cultural knowledge, the theoretical knowledge of developmental possibilities, and the knowledge or experience of organizations. Given area specialization and a broad appreciation of the culture where extension work is to be carried out, the anthropologist needs to educate himself in terms of the remaining two categories. But, assuming this training, what is he then to do?

He begins by being aware of the cultural milieu or, more specifically, of the people's existing horizon of experience, the kinds of things they want or dislike, the goals they seek, and their view of the innovating organization. He can then take a close look at the design and operation of the existing extension program. In the nonspecialized area of his training he has become aware of the technical requirements and possibilities of the situation. His advice is structured in such a way as to mediate between the old and the new, the social concomitants and the civil service requirements. Such an anthropologist is sensitive to the anthropology not only of his people but also of the innovating organization.

Rather than continuing to regard himself solely as a professional anthropologist sensitive to the powers, privileges, and immunities of an academic milieu he becomes cognizant of and sensitive to the demands of the broader scene in terms of planning and execution. It is, of course, vital that the development anthropologist be possessed of those necessary human qualities which enable him to cooperate with other professionals. A senior academic is not always a useful development worker.

VII

The Nonexpert Side of the Expert
in Advisory Work

Development anthropologists must familiarize themselves with the way governments and international agencies work. Principles of advisory work are probably no more scientific than principles of anthropological fieldwork, though successful completion of both requires attention to detail. However, because of what one could term a 'philosopher king' tradition in applied anthropology it is important to assert that academic issues and concerns are tangential—insofar as research and publication are stressed—to public affairs where results must be achieved.

George Foster believes that academics make good applied people [1] Do professors of medicine make good general practitioners? What is required to apply knowledge usefully is quite different from what is required to undertake and publish research. The personal outlook, commitment, philosophy, goals, satisfactions, techniques, methods, and training ought to be recognized as being quite distinct. Indeed, it seems scarcely credible that applied anthropologists feel that there can be such easy movement between the university and outside work.

1. *Applied Anthropology*, Boston, 1969, pp. 39–54.

It is important for anthropologists to recognize nonexpert aspects of advisory work. By this I mean an examination of things and issues not normally dealt with in the literature. For example, attention must be given to the expert as a person and not just as a scholar: interaction with other specialists and nonspecialists determines not only the kind of report that will be written but also at times the way the report will be received. If the over-all effectiveness of advisory work is to be evaluated and appreciated, consideration must be given to the 'nuts and bolts' of advice, the selection of experts, their terms of reference, briefing, fact finding procedures, reporting, and the reception of expert opinion by the government or agency recommended to take action by the analyses. This all requires knowledge and experience which academics do not normally possess.[2]

It is a common error to expect too much of experts. Governments, faced with legislation on tax reform which seems impossibly difficult to draft, with the need to stimulate the sluggish agricultural sector of the economy, or with other exceedingly complex issues, often have a tendency to imagine that their problems would vanish if only an expert would appear. The film *South Pacific* may have said that if you never had a dream you would never have a dream come true, but experts do not always make dreams come true.[3]

When an international agency or even a government department receives a request for research to be undertaken, a deci-

2. See the papers in *Institutions and the Person*, H. Becker *et al.* (eds.), Chicago, 1968, and P. Hammond (ed.), *Sociologists at Work*, New York, 1968. D. Lerner and W. Schramm, *Communications and Change in the Developing Countries*, Honolulu, 1967, has no guidance nor does I. Swerdlow (ed.), *Development Administration*, Syracuse, 1963; the economist D. Seers "Why Visiting Economists Fail," *Journal of Political Economy*, August 1962, has valuable hints. The Peace Corps has made a relevant approach; see H. Cleveland, G. J. Mangone, and J. C. Adams, *The Overseas Americans*, New York, 1960. An early classic is H. J. Laski, *The Limitations of the Expert*, London, 1931. Most of the literature concentrates on helping the expert to do his job more effectively but implicitly ignores the 'gray area' I deal with here. However, it does seem odd that much attention should be paid to the community development worker as a person and little attention paid to experts as persons.

3. Seers, *"Visiting Economists"*; Albert Waterston, *Development Planning; The Lessons of Experience*, Baltimore, 1965, p. 365.

sion must be made on whether or not the requirement is to be met from within the organization or let out on a contract basis. This is no easy decision. The likely demands of research must be matched against the operational capacity of staff members and the degree of inconvenience that might possibly ensue if key personnel were absent for a short or long period of time. The engagement of research workers on short-term contract terms of service as a practice has several advantages. The agency can supply individual researchers of high calibre. The team can be tailored to research specifications. Short-term researchers can all be taken from one country, thus getting over the nationality quota problem—a troublesome problem for international agencies [4]—so all that has to be done is to ensure that each of the team members is acceptable to the government of the country where research will be carried out.

Where short-term assignments are concerned—and it is those that I am concerned with here—the selection process is not very democratic. In foreign ministries of western Europe, and North America, civil servants in charge of recruitment for international agencies make it their business to keep in touch with a few key figures in the academic world. These professors can be relied upon to produce qualified individuals for short-term assignments at short notice. In some cases people in other branches of government will have placed their names on waiting lists for international appointments. Recruitment for international agencies is not advertised widely—personal contact is the keynote.

This is true, for example, in Britain where the International Recruitment Unit for the Ministry of Overseas Development keeps a roster of experts who can be called on at short notice for short-term and permanent appointment. One has to know that this roster exists in order to get on it. I know of one officer who got himself in the unit, watched the jobs go by, picked one, and is now in Washington. The 'backstairs' approach is not very good for the image of the international agencies.

A drawback of this short-term recruitment system is the fact that few people anywhere in the process have an overview, so

4. See H. G. Nicholson, *The United Nations as a Political Institution*, New York, 1967.

they cannot check the predatory expansion of some disciplines or suggest the possible utility of others. There are too few civil servants in the international agencies qualified in terms of background and experience to say to the ministry of foreign affairs in X country or the professor of a famous university: "Look, do you think that this is really what we need?" In selecting experts or even in deciding if they should be selected it is vital for the international civil servant to have a 'generalizing capacity,' i.e., a broad knowledge of disciplines, and a broad experience of development. After all a civil servant who has only been trained as an economist is hardly likely to say boo to a famous economist.[5]

Something more on this. In Britain, for example, Colonial Office personnel had an appreciation of what anthropology could do, but many senior officers in the Foreign Office or Commonwealth Relations Office have had no training in the subject and have very little idea of anthropology's potential utility. I have found the same ignorance among international agency personnel, for frequently these people are simply former metropolitan civil servants or executives from business who have had no specialized training for development work. They suffer some of the same handicaps as applied anthropologists in that they do not know sufficiently well what could be done. They know a good deal about organization though little about the importance of cultural variation. This Westernized experience and training leads them naturally to emphasize economics, education, and agriculture. Large issues are examined and explored, and anthropology appears to have little to recommend it.

Where anthropologists have been engaged on short-term assignments this, to me, seems to have denoted patronage rather

5. T. Balogh, *The Economics of Poverty*, Bristol, 1966, p. 324, and "The Apotheosis of the Dilettante" in H. Dalton (ed.), *The Establishment*, London, 1959, suggests that good civil servants possess well-developed dialectical powers rather than knowledge about the world. Writers on public administration have made the same criticism (C. H. Sisson, *The Spirit of British Administration*, London, 1959, pp. 23, 24). "The public administrator becomes a kind of ringmaster and strategist combined who must not only direct his program but also win support for it from the legislature, from his own employees, from the public served, and from other governmental agencies that must be satisfied" (M. E. Dimock, G. O. Dimock, and L. W. Koenig, *Public Administration*, New York, 1960, p. 37).

than a desire to re-examine policy. However, given the outlook and training of most applied anthropologists, a fundamental change could not have been expected.

Terms of reference given an expert may in themselves be an expression of policy rather than an invitation to research. The way in which the problem is posed to the expert will determine to some extent the possible range of responses. A national agency may draw up terms of reference for all projects in a similar way; governments may set up terms of reference as a political defense mechanism. It is important for the expert to know what he is accepting; he ought not to think always that he knows better than his clients and that his only duty is to be a scientist and produce the 'truth.'

Inevitably the truth will have to comprehend not only the technical sphere of the expert but the prevailing political and social milieu. The terms of reference will not tell this, only experience and the results of thorough investigation can produce it. The terms of reference that are given an expert are a kind of symbolic recognition of this specialty and the kinds of things that his profession does; using these guidelines, adjusting, manipulating, negotiating so that the expert can achieve the most satisfying professional response means an expedition into the nonexpert 'gray' area.

Development of personal sensitivity in this area is an administrative rather than an academic art—for this reason it is dangerous to pluck an academic, no matter how senior, from a background where he is aware only of university politics, and deposit him in the civil service milieu where things are very different though the need for competence in negotiating, for instance, is no less important. It may be advisable for the individual professional to give his opinion on policy from time to time but if he does not appreciate how the policy is made and changed then this may be a fairly pointless exercise for expert and government alike.

All this might appear very 'common sensical' but it is important to say these things because there are quite contrary notions of the proper role of the expert floating round in academic circles. In the first section of *Applied Sociology*, A. Gouldner, one of the editors, puts forward a social science viewpoint. His notion is based on a set of related concepts about social science and the nature of institutions. They come to the conclusion that clients may not even appreciate their *real* problems and that they may, albeit unconsciously, 'resist' the 'correct' courses of action recommended by the social scientists. I believe this to be dangerous.

My concern is not so much with the fact that these may be logically interrelated statements ultimately susceptible to empirical verification but rather with the 'omniscience' pretensions of this approach. For here the sociologist is, in effect, saying he is *the* one who knows and he is right. This is the very form of reasoning which led early anthropologists to suppose that through sociological analysis alone they could produce valuable statements about economics, for instance.

Therefore, in terms of the categories I introduced earlier, I doubt the appropriateness of this view of the expert. If a theory is built entirely of sociological bits and pieces and then tested in the same manner it may well appear to be scientifically correct. But then the recommendations must also fall within the ambit of sociological experience. Analysis of a social situation is a vital tool, but its utility is dependent upon consideration of the right kinds of facts and experience. And right solutions are more a matter of ideology than science. After all if Gouldner and Miller were asked to consider a development problem they would come up with one solution, but, are we to believe that the solutions of other social scientists from other disciplines would be the same as theirs?

The scholarly procedure, surely, is to consider the widest range of facts, theories, and concepts. Considering the problems, what grounds are there for continuing the university division of labor? I do not see the time when social scientists can assume, in terms of the perspective afforded by a single discipline, that they are 'right' and anyone who 'resists' has some kind of psychological 'twitch.' If Gouldner and Miller were 'right,' the world would be run by sociologists. I am quite glad it is not.

Fact finding on an assignment or mission must be comprehensive; it must extend into the nonexpert area. There are very superior experts, celestial creatures, who descend to deliver expertise and jet back whence they came. Lesser experts reside in 'specialist ghettoes' while the information they need is being produced, or they join the local civil service. Here, as I said before, I am concerned with some of the problems posed by demands for information at short notice.

Individualism, and independence, during a fact-finding mission tend to lower the standing of an expert and may easily prejudice his work. An individual (or group) who comes and lives alone with his thoughts and then returns to draw up a report has probably done a less than satisfactory job. During the fact-finding phase an expert must become as far as possible a functioning member of the local civil service; he needs to know the personnel so that he appreciates their ability and capacity to do things. More importantly, he needs to get to know the people. These things help to inject reality into a plan. The host country may have provided a tour, arranged stopovers, and so on. All too often the only local people the expert meets are servants or selected individuals who often perform in a highly structured context.

Do I deny the value and strength of the anthropological fieldwork tradition? In a way I do. The impression given by the literature [6] is that the fieldwork of the applied and the academic anthropologist are quite similar. This is a very unrealistic assessment. Traditional fieldwork techniques and methods are often going to be of limited utility in development work.

In the first place let us consider the time element. Authorities will often be unable to wait for the length of time it normally takes an anthropologist to collect his data. Second, one must consider its representativeness, a problem I have touched on several times: how valuable is a community study going to be to those concerned with national policy? Third, the researcher is often going to be associated with authority, a state of affairs fieldworkers have traditionally attempted to avoid. All of this demands, if anthropologists are to meet administrative deadlines and sudden requests for information in times of crisis, a

6. See, for example, Foster, *Applied Anthropology*, pp. 66–71.

thorough mastery of the literature that is available, the use of knowledge gained from experience, and judgment, in an attempt to satisfy the three categories I have mentioned. Economists do not usually have the statistical data they require in order to be completely scholarly and academic, and with respect to cultural data anthropologists are often going to be in the same position. A completely new anthropological approach to data collection is required.

Assuming that the anthropologist is an area specialist, that he knows what could be done, and also has knowledge of organizational delivery systems, what then? One may not have time for comprehensive work, and the traditional approach would seem impossible. Development proposals can be monitored for cultural 'fit.' Then it is probably going to be necessary for the anthropologist to arrive in the field with a number of specific theoretical ideas and to have these tested.

Rapport may never be established. Resentment has often arisen among local civil servants as a consequence of the expert's concern with his terms and conditions of service. One U.N.E.S.C.O. adviser I knew on the teaching of English as a second language was not as competent as a local officer receiving a fourteenth of the expert's salary. Sometimes after the receiving country has agreed to provide a house, servants, office, and transport for the expert, he arrives to find none of these things available. Justifiably annoyed, he complains, and, as he pries each of the promised things from the local administration, he succeeds in emphasizing the luxury of his own circumstances, and the fact that as an individual he appears more concerned with his own comfort than the job. Technical people, for example, are often less than tactful when they demand their legitimate pound of flesh from the local government. It is a simple though common facet of human nature that if a man is not liked or respected then people will look closely at what the man has to say, being quite ready to take him up on the smallest and least important matter, and being delighted if they can fault his work.

The development anthropologist may be associated with an

agency or government that is unpopular. Early anthropological monographs often give the impression that the fieldworker somehow felt that he was invisible; contemporary research focuses much more on the observer making an objective assessment of the extent to which his presence may distort the data. In both positions there is a degree of neutrality, a degree of noninvolvement, so that even with the most modern fieldwork theories there tends to be an assumption of neutrality. It is the analytical rather than the personal role that is emphasized. This is believed to be a necessary position if sensitive and confidential information is to be collected. Vital, if the researcher is to move freely among factions or communities. For the development anthropologist things are more difficult.

The mission member is more visible in every sense than the traditional fieldworker; the fact of employment is indicative of the exercise of certain value choices; his work is definitely going to affect people. An academic is reasonably free to choose which facts he will consider, whereas the existence of public feeling may place pressure on the development anthropologist to justify his consideration of certain facts and omission of others. The personality of the man suddenly becomes of more importance than the character of his science. When matters of immediate concern are breached, the general public, no matter in what society, is not inclined to support the idea that there is such a thing as a disinterested social science.

For the expert collecting facts there is a need for *diplomacy*, seldom emphasized, because people seem to think that diplomacy is something practiced only by diplomats. This is not the case. Diplomacy is a good way of doing business, a compound of common sense and experience which has evolved through the years with the object of minimizing the harmful potential of nonexpert relations. I am not suggesting that all experts should become diplomats. I am suggesting that it would be useful to look for certain qualities in an expert, even when chosen for a short-term assignment, and that the provision of some quasi-diplomatic training or advice for experts might be valuable.

The existence of friction in university departments and the experiences of graduate students indicate that the professional anthropologist is not, by virtue of his study, any more gifted in personal relationships than other mortals.

There is a need to emphasize calm, patience, good temper, modesty, and loyalty.[7] Teamwork is no less important. These are not only the qualities of a diplomat; they lie at the heart of good extension work. Experts often overlook these points, often appearing to believe that technical proficiency is the most important thing and that they should "call the shots as they see them." The history of applied anthropology is a good indication why experts should not behave in this way. Texts on applied anthropology (and sociology) imply that anthropologists are fairly perfect human beings who have little to learn from other disciplines or professions. The expert, these texts suggest, should not regard himself as responsible to his agency or civil service employees but to his fellow anthropologists and his 'science.' The result is a sad situation where applied anthropologists cannot understand why they should not be free to criticize administrators and why again the international agencies virtually ignore anthropology. This demonstrates the dangers of trying to turn the developing countries into an extension of a university department.

The impression given by an expert during fact finding is of the utmost importance. This impression may carry considerable weight when the completed report is received. It is important to stress this because anthropologists do not have, as a class, a very distinguished record in this sphere. At this point the civil service is supreme, and civil servants are unlikely to do something just because X urges it from a point of view of orthodoxy, especially if one or two ministers found X a rather tiresome person. An economist who puts people's backs up may achieve less in the long run than a man who carries local opinion with him. Flexibility, hard work, a good head for alcohol, and a fund of anecdotes are probably of more importance than a long list of publications that few civil servants will bother to read or try to understand.[8]

7. Sir Ernest Satow, *Guide to Diplomatic Practice*, London, 1932.
8. Sisson, *Spirit of British Administration*, pp. 23–37.

A danger is that most civil servants are used to assuming that an expert is competent. If he were not they assume he would not have been sent. So that a great deal is inevitably placed on personality when civil servants assess the value of expert advice. A man who has not troubled to hide his disdain for lowly administrators, and who then finds after he has made his survey that he has to recommend an unpleasant course of action is straining things. The expert who has taken the trouble to find out how things work locally and who recommends a tough course of action is in a better position because it is probable that the senior civil servants will feel that the man made a good impression all the way up the line.

Due to exigencies of time and space the allocation of effort during fact collection on an advisory mission is, as I have suggested, a more sensitive and delicate task than traditional fieldwork. A number of suggestions can be made. The length of time spent collecting data is no small consideration. While it is important not to reject the advice of senior officials in the capital, it is also vital to get out to the rural areas. There the officials will not only probably be pleased to see a visiting expert but only too glad to put across their point of view without 'vetting' by senior civil servants in the capital. Perspective will be added, not only because of the things seen and new people met, but because it will increase the expert's feel for the situation and he will not then easily succumb to taking the advice of urban officials who may well be out of touch. From such visits stems a more accurate appreciation of the service and the country as a whole, and a report can then be tailored to fit the capacity that exists, and perhaps even the tensions that are to be seen between rural areas and the capital.[9]

Commercial people and government people in rural areas are unlikely to tell an expert all they know at first meeting—they naturally worry lest this might be repeated verbatim in the capital. As a junior officer I remember meeting 'high powered' visiting experts who asked me what I thought. I seldom said very much since the experts were destined to return straight to the

9. Waterston, *Development Planning*, p. 288.

capital to confer with my superiors. Alternatively a visiting United Nations economist who spent a convivial evening in the local club impressed a friend and me so much that we devoted a day to showing him what the territory was *really* like. In 'normal' circumstances an anthropologist can guard against these dangers because he can spend a fair amount of time in his community. But on a mission things are tremendously speeded up. One must accept that fieldwork may not be of a very high standard.

The anthropologist need not assume the sole burden for fact collection. It is in his interest to coordinate his research design and inquiry with those of other mission members. The more ideas, viewpoints, shared experiences, among mission members the better. What is required is not so much kinds of information directed toward the concerns of anthropology as data of relevance to the total effort of the mission.

A good report will not only be clearly written but it will have appraised local needs and local capacity to meet these needs to the extent that a positive contribution to development will be made by the plan. It will not merely be strong criticism of current practices. A good report will spell out in fair detail what ought to be done rather than making a blanket suggestion from behind the authority of the mission or expert. It will not deal with contentious matters and personalities in a way which might give offense to serving officials, and sources of sensitive information will not be identified.[10]

Walinsky has given an admirable outline of the informational characteristics of a high quality report: "(It) is *clear* because it is understandable to those who must use it; *timely* because it gets to them when they need it; *reliable* because *diverse* observers using the same procedures see it in the same way; *valid* because it is cast in the form of concepts and measures that capture reality; *adequate* because the account is full; and *wide-ranging* because the major policy alternatives promising a

10. The ideal report does not judge, evaluate, or criticize existing efforts; it gives the facts and then makes recommendations. See Mary Parker Follett, "The Illusion of Final Authority," *Bulletin of the Taylor Society*, XI (October 1926).

high probability of attaining organizational goals are posed or new goals suggested." [11] This statement in itself is a powerful critique of applied anthropology. Many anthropological accounts are unduly 'jargonized' and hard for laymen to understand; the delay between fieldwork and analysis is often excessive; there may be little agreement among anthropologists regarding the appropriateness of recommendations; applied anthropology has only dwelt on an aspect of development reality; the accounts are not full because the innovating organization is ignored; and the major policy alternatives are not set out. Development anthropology has a long way to go before it becomes useful. It is not enough to talk about applying knowledge. There must emerge a much more pragmatic idea of how and why this is done in development work.

Reports are required which dovetail into the local development situation. Recognition is made of how things are seen by those who will have to implement the plan; the character of the local people who will have to live under the plan has been catered for; and the demands which will be made on the government (if this should be accepted) have been assessed in human as well as monetary terms. Reports which are suppressed, rejected, unacceptable, widely modified, or 'commissioned' or 'inquired' to death, may be truthful, may be technically excellent, but, *prima facie*, they are evidence that the man has not done his homework on the nonexpert side.

It is sometimes better to get a little done than nothing at all.

Social scientists have got to accept academic shortfalls in the real world. Conditions will never be ideal, and the only place for a full-blown, fully matured concept of academic freedom is the university. To achieve progress there must always be compromise, and by this I do not mean that one can hope to be academic and practical at the same time. I may appear to labor this point in an irritating manner though I do so only because I find the continual extolling of academic virtues a consistently and dangerously naïve element in most applied texts.

The development anthropologist is going to be subject to au-

11. H. J. Walinsky, *Organizational Intelligence: Knowledge and Policy in Government and Industry*, New York, 1967, viii, ix.

thority. If he disagrees, he can resign. But if he does not accept the principle and continues to think of a higher academic loyalty, then he has no place in government or in an international agency. It is the administrator, who has the training and the responsibility to weigh the evidence and the opinions of social scientists, who is charged with decision-making. Too often applied anthropologists give the impression they feel themselves qualified to possess a decision-making capacity that they are not entitled to in their own country.

Some experts think that their report is the most important aspect of the assignment, a closely guarded secret like the shape of next year's model car. Then, when this report has been submitted, they feel that their responsibilities are at an end. It is much better if some attempt is made to discuss tentative recommendations locally. If the expert stresses at the time that these are only ideas going through his mind it is more than likely that he will be able to gauge possible local reaction, correct factual errors and wrong assumptions, and take into account details which he may have ignored. And it is not entirely satisfactory to do this with senior civil servants, or heads of government, just before departing. Lesser ranking civil servants are likely to feel good things about being brought into the expert's confidence at all stages of the mission. Situations arise where everyone is waiting for a report like an examination result. Then when the report is received the expert is not in the country or has left for his next assignment. These situations, in my opinion, have been badly managed.

The expert himself needs to be a teacher, not just a lecturer. In many cases where the expert has not established very close contact with civil servants in the host government the report is received and for a time no person seems to have a very clear idea of what ought to be done. The body of the document may be split up into a large number of files for individual 'action,' especially where criticism of existing government policy is concerned. It is unwise to offer strong criticism of a government, because much time may be spent thinking up possible defenses or possible answers to nasty questions in 'the house' or the legislature.

If there is no organizing theme in the report then each section may be farmed out to the officer with agriculture, natural resources, or other administrative responsibilities. He then liaises with his opposite numbers in the technical ministry. All of this uses time and weakens the prospects for implementation. Alternatively, an independent treasury can easily declare a report unsound without going into too much detail. And, to imply that the course of action suggested would be politically inappropriate—though the researcher could not have been expected to be aware of this—is the kind of 'fast ball' that few international agencies are able to field.

Senior civil servants can emasculate virtually any report that they dislike strongly.[12] This is hard reality. Politicians may do what they please but somehow things just do not work out. Even where a report has the provisional support of all sections in the developing country while the expert is present, there may still be problems. An expert report needs expert assessment and expert knowledge for implementation.

A single expert either reporting or assessing has a limited utility in any development situation. This has obvious implications for anthropologists who often view their applied work in isolation from the needs and concerns of other development workers. For yet another of the sins of neglecting nonexpert skills is the denial of Parkinson's Law.

Let me summarize. There are dangers inherent in engaging experts, particularly from the universities, on short-term assignments with no experience of government or agency work. Failure in the 'nonexpert' sphere could imperil the technical aspect of a mission. Pitfalls might be avoided through adherence to fairly common sense rules. If agencies and governments are prepared to invest heavily in the engagement of 'experts' then they should take the extra precaution of selecting men with an eye to nonexpert attributes. Experts should be given some kind of orientation course which would not only dwell on the culture horrors—i.e., when to burp and when not to, when not to eat pork, when to wear shoes,—but would also deal with the structure of the receiving government's civil service and how things get done there.

12. G. E. Strauss, *The Ruling Servants*, London, 1961, and E. N. Gladden, *The Essentials of Public Administration*, 1961 ed., give a number of examples.

VIII

Economists and Development Planning

Economic development, in the sense that the term is used by economists, has largely been ignored by applied anthropologists. It is to authors such as Firth, Belshaw, and Salisbury (see bibliography) that we must give the credit for any advances that have been achieved. Academically, economic anthropologists show an ability to achieve a much deeper appreciation of the functioning of peasant and 'primitive' economic systems than could be achieved by anthropology or economics alone. Economic anthropology has been making gigantic strides in recent years and if current progress is maintained it should not be too long before governments and international agencies actively recognize—a number of social scientists now do—the vital dimension that anthropology could add to the planning process. However, there are still a number of development planners who see economists going it alone.

Economists have devoted painfully little time to their mandates for allocation.[1] It is, I think, stretching the imagination to suggest that the restructuring of society has little to do with 'morality,' and few anthropologists would agree with this posi-

1. Albert Waterston in his account of the World Bank's experience, *Development Planning; The Lessons of Experience*, Baltimore, 1965, pp. 8, 9.

tion. People all over the world are having their lives affected to varying degrees by the prescriptions of development economists, and it is of the utmost importance to examine this notion of a value-free science, free from ethnocentrism, because it simply allocates in order to secure the maximum economic advantage.

When we examine the notion that the economist is simply attempting to make the most advantageous allocation, being solely concerned with the relationship between means and ends, we see immediate difficulties. For example, there is a lively debate on whether or not education ought to be considered an investment.[2] The idea that one can plan an educational system, gearing the kinds of education to the types of manpower needed at a particular time but without any sense of moral purpose, is an odd one. Another example is in the sphere of fiscal policy. Fiscal measures are sometimes designed to force participation in a market economy.[3] The assumption is that involvement with a Western money economy will succeed in establishing a new pattern of preferences.[4] A few economists have handed out these doses of medicine to a wide number of countries, a practice that has caused colleagues to accuse them of 'quackery.'[5] These are, of course, extreme examples, and, though they illustrate dangers, they could not be held representative of development economists in general. And such issues are ignored in anthropology.

However, I would maintain that there is a certain lack of sensitivity toward social issues among economists who have ignored the relevance of anthropology. Little attention has been paid to what the people themselves might actually want. Nor is there any systematic attempt to find out how the people themselves would like to participate in the growth process.[6] This should be of the utmost *practical* importance. I don't think I'm

2. These issues are discussed in T. Balogh, *The Economics of Poverty*, Bristol, 1966, pp. 103–104. A different view is given by T. W. Schultz, *The Economic Value of Education*, New York, 1963.
3. N. Kaldor, "Will Underdeveloped Countries Learn to Tax?" *Foreign Affairs*, January 1963.
4. J. S. G. Wilson, *An Economic Survey of the New Hebrides*, London, 1965.
5. D. Seers, "Why Visiting Economists Fail," *Journal of Political Economy*, August 1962.
6. Waterston, *Development Planning*

preaching to the converted; books on development economics
mention little anthropology; books on economic anthropology
have little to say about development economics.

A difference exists between a self-regulating market economy
and an economy which is regulated by government interven-
tion.[7] Import quotas, export bonuses or taxes, licenses, personal
and business taxation are a consequence of advice received from
economists. Choice of projects may be hard, or choice of sectors
for investment may be hard, but in all cases there is a selective
process for projects, and a ranking system for their evaluation.
Choice involves the exercise of values by the economist which
are not always related to economy or efficiency. Selection of
what to maximize or what to minimize is always linked to values, and the values of the economist are not always going to be
those of the people he seeks to aid.

Economists working in the developing countries can often ab-
rogate to themselves the right to determine the nature of the development process in a country, the way of life that the people
must be persuaded to adopt as a consequence, and the length of
time that this process should take. Privately, some economists
pay attention to the importance of cultural variation, but this
also needs to be emphasized in some of the development economics literature. For example, the economist Kindleberger says:
"There is enough in economic development for sociologists and
economists to study in their own disciplines without the need to
argue the primacy of one subject over another . . . It is entirely
understandable if the psychologists, psychiatrists, sociologists,
and cultural anthropologists proclaim the dominance of cultural
and social aspects over the economic. This attitude is to be expected and conveys no information." [8] The issue is not one of
primacy but one of recognition.

Development economists admit that theories about how
growth takes place are fragmentary.[9] Statistics, particularly, are
seldom satisfactory in a developing country—or in many ad-

7. See W. Firey, *Law and Economy in Planning*, Austin, 1965.
8. Kindleberger, *Economic Development*, New York, 1965, pp. 38–39, 18.
9. Waterston, *Development Planning*, p. 7; A. K. Cairncross, *Factors in
Economic Development*, London, 1962, pp. 272–291.

vanced economies for that matter—and it will be a matter of
some years before adequate records can be obtained.[10] So it is
hard to construct reliable mathematical models. But even among
economists themselves there is growing appreciation that where
model building has been attempted, sums *alone* are inadequate
because no matter how elegantly they solve a problem or point
to a fruitful course of action, the answer must be determined by
real life situations which often turn out to be very different.[11]
'Econopoly,' the domination of development planning by economists, may not be the best solution. Anthropologists who feel
that administrators dominate planning should read some development economics.

Since there is no single way to achieve growth, the planning
process is often reduced to a matter of opinion. There is no sure
way of knowing what will happen, how people will react, how
events will change. A good plan remains fairly flexible, it has
built-in recognition of the fact that planning is largely a process
of trial and error. Some economists admit that there is nothing
very abstruse or difficult about theory underlying the planning
process.[12] It does seem important, in making a plea for more interdisciplinary work, to stress (a) that economists do not have
any comprehensive theory to cover the social change process
that a few claim pre-eminence in administering, and (b) that
despite the elegance and complexity of mathematical models they
have been rejected by many economists because they are non-
operational. But despite all this, Waterston of the World Bank
maintains that "since the core of a central planning agency's
work is to ascertain choices for using resources, a task which is
basically economic, a planning agency's greatest need is for
economists." [13]

The strength of an economic adviser lies in his familiarity
with the kinds of data he works with; he can recognize signs

10. P. Bauer and B. Yamey, *The Economies of Underdeveloped Countries*,
London, 1957; Waterston, *Development Planning*, pp. 198–200.
11. H. Morganstern, *On the Accuracy of Economic Observations*, Princeton, 1963; D. Riesman, "The Suburban Dislocation," *The Annals of the
American Academy of Political Science*, November 1967.
12. Cairncross, *Factors*, pp. 272–291.
13. Waterston, *Development Planning*, p. 517.

and indications of things that are happening or about to happen; he has developed judgment and a feel for the situation; his analysis may be more careful and his proposals more comprehensive than those who are not schooled in his discipline.[14] Interpretation is often a matter of general knowledge. In a development situation the economist alone may not always have this general knowledge. E. E. Hagen makes the admission that "economic development also requires human qualities that we do not know how to affect."[15] Lord Balogh, for example, makes several references in his book on development economics to the fact that a particular plan was poor 'sociology.'[16] But in Waterston's authoritative exposition of the World Bank's planning experience the need for anthropology or sociology is not even mentioned.[17]

Economists do not sufficiently appreciate that there is a difference between providing means for people to improve their personal material positions in life, means which they need not accept, and providing means which must be accepted because they must be applied in a predetermined manner.

Economists can dictate that airports be of a certain construction, that indigenous housing be of a certain design,[18] that children in schools learn certain subjects. But there is a difference between an objective set of criteria for annual growth, and the subjective image that people themselves may have of their circumstances.[19] This important distinction is something that economists are, I think, not themselves equipped to handle through training or experience. It is vital that development planners

14. Cairncross, Factors, pp. 271–292.
15. The Economics of Development, Cambridge, Mass., 1968, p. 484.
16. Economics of Poverty.
17. Waterston, Development Planning. Nor is the position any different in the country surveys by I.R.B.D. published for the Bank by the Johns Hopkins Press, Baltimore.
18. See, for example, The Economic Development of the Territory of Papua and New Guinea, issued by an I.R.B.D. mission, Baltimore, 1965, pp. 354–361. Incidentally, this report completely ignores the work of the Australian National University's New Guinea Research Unit. (The unit's first Bulletin was published in April 1963.)
19. H. Myint, The Economics of Developing Countries, London, 1965, p. 19, makes this valuable point.

help here. Economies of what and for what is a cultural rather than a purely mathematical problem.

Criticism of development economics can, I think, be justified when we find some economists who claim omniscience when they allocate. These economists would appear to ignore the fact that economic decisions affect social development—and vice versa. Economic and social aspects of reality are inseparable.[20] The kinds of information an anthropologist can supply could be very useful to the economist. Some economists, realizing that something has to be done to improve prediction, have decided to "leave the rigor of economic models and turn to economic history, sociology, and personality theory."[21] We can work together with value profiles; we can find out what people think and want, and what they say they are likely to do; we can translate what might be done into terms which real people understand; and we can think of ways in which they can let us know what they would like to be done. We have no magic but it is probably better to have this information than not.

Anthropologists know a good deal about real people, though their theories of change are fragmentary; economists know a good deal about economizing in the substantive sense, and would perhaps be more effective if they took account of real people. Neither side has any magic. But cultural knowledge of a people and knowledge of an economic process should, if joined, be an effective combination. Anthropologists know where people have come from in terms of their cultural antecedents, economists know where people could end up in terms of their economic future, and what is needed from both disciplines is a contribution for the present. As Malinowski wrote in his introduction to H. I. Hogbin's *Law and Order in Polynesia* (London, 1934, xxxi): "Never . . . forget the living, palpitating flesh and blood organism of man which remains somewhere at the heart of every institution." Another comment by an anthropologist is also relevant: "When, however, economic theory moves from the realm of pure abstraction to analysis and description of the be-

20. Waterston, *Development Planning*, p. 528.
21. Hagen, *Economics of Development*, p. 481.

haviour of people in any specific society, then additional assumptions must be inserted into the argument. The objection that can be legitimately raised against some aspects of economic analysis is that such assumptions, which should be explicit and based upon empirical study, are often only half explored and based upon some vague general notions of what is the local norm of behavior . . . how does one arrive at the idea that it is good or correct to assume a regularity in the system of wants? Only ultimately from some observation of the behavior of people." [22]

If the *aid-givers* stipulate that anthropological research is a necessary and useful part of project feasibility studies, preliminary planning, and re-evaluation processes, then it will be done. 'Banker's rules' operate in this connection. The banker sets conditions, and recognition of anthropology is hardly likely to cause great fuss.

This whole area shows what can happen when we stop assuming that the whole world can be interpreted according to the canons of anthropological research. I do not think anyone could claim that applied anthropologists played a major, or even a minor, role in this progress. And the question is raised as to why similar developments have not taken place with respect to agriculture, education, and law for instance. Though I believe the need to be great, I do not deal with agriculture or education here, though I hope to in the near future. Instead I have a few observations to make on legal matters. We go from the brightest prospect in the anthropology of development to the most dismal view.

22. R. Firth, *The Elements of Social Organization*, 2nd ed., Boston, 1964, pp. 128, 129.

IX

Legal Anthropology: The Need for an Anglo-American Legal Dimension

Recent intellectual ferment in the anthropological profession has stressed that academics ought to be more 'concerned,' that their knowledge ought to produce some positive benefit. Can the kinds of knowledge necessary for social amelioration be derived from conventional academic inquiry? Or, put another way, can conventional academic inquiry be carried on in the processes of social amelioration? Anyone wishing, for example, to explore the ways in which anthropological knowledge could assist in the revision, drafting, or understanding of the kinds of legislation called for by modernization or even the preservation of a distinctive cultural heritage has no substantial foundation on which to build.

Why should this be? One reason might be thought to lie in the fact that few anthropologists have had formal legal training; another, in the fact that the kinds of things studied by anthropologists have been far removed from the legislative process. Neither reason fits the facts adequately. But to get the facts one must see what has been done on the purely academic side, to see whether or not a concerned research strategy would require a radical departure from existing practice.

I want to indicate several weaknesses in the ethnography of law, and make some recommendations for the development of the subject. I want to examine the kinds of information that are useful to the lawyer and at the same time to indicate how greater cooperation between the two professions might help to make development and academic work more effective.

The legal anthropologists' obsession with model building and comparative work has, I think, preceded satisfactory analysis of particular societies and their law. I concentrate on the work of Pospisil and Hoebel (see bibliography) since it is fairly representative of what legal anthropologists have been trying to do. Most of the enterprise in the ethnography of law has been of a presumed legal situation which anthropologists have tried to explain by using an ideal type. Anthropological monographs on law tend to have, as a primary aim, verification of the particular author's definition of what constitutes law. My concern, looking at legal anthropology, must, therefore, begin with models of law or universalistic definitions of law in terms of their legal and anthropological validity.

It is surely necessary for legal anthropologists to study more law than they have done. Why has legal anthropology been so little influenced by Anglo-American law? While one cannot expect legal anthropologists, as a class, to have the professional competence of a lawyer, one can reasonably ask that when anthropologists use terms which have precise and special meanings for lawyers, they take the trouble to acquaint themselves with these special meanings. Terms like theft, contract, tort, and homicide are used in a very loose way by anthropologists without any real attempt systematically to define and order their constituent elements.

It will continue to be hard for legal anthropologists to know when their comments, on their own or others' law, are either original, valid, or useful, until they do the necessary legal homework. Anthropologists, widely thought of as knowing about law, have evidently not studied very much law, or at least not understood it. We must spend some time examining the 'universalistic' law definitions of Hoebel and Pospisil. Anthropologists have not gained any systematic appreciation of the development of Western legal analysis. Criminal law, evidence, contract, torts, and administrative law, in the sense that these branches of law are understood and used in our courts, find no systematic or rigorous expression in the work of legal anthropologists. Indeed, little attempt has been made to examine the potential utility of Anglo-American law. Even for Gluckman, the most perceptive of the legal anthropologists, the need to incorporate the approaches of Western lawyers is at best a profession of faith, like the need to conduct interdisciplinary research. He never really gets down to it. It is not too harsh a verdict to conclude that the main utility of Anglo-American legal concepts has been the supply of chapter headings, such as "Criminal Law" and "Civil Law" in books written by legal anthropologists.

Hogbin and Schapera [1] provide good examples of what I mean. There is really no attempt, as Laura Nader suggested when she surveyed the field generally,[2] to contrast the various aspects of the primitive system against the "familiar backdrop of Western European Law." It seems fairly pointless to set up chapters with headings such as "Criminal Law" suggesting that the Anglo-American legal 'backdrop' is to be used, when during the ensuing exposition it is obvious that the writer has only a vague idea about what our law is in the West. The facts are not only of omission—there is also unwarranted presumption. Hoebel and Pospisil [3] begin by saying how a definition of law has eluded legal scholars through the ages and then, rather modestly, each shows how he, and anthropology, has a 'working definition.' Anthropology is for these authors, *the* way of looking at things; readers are given the impression that a careful analysis of Anglo-American categories of law, though commendably erudite, is not really necessary for legal analysis of primitive societies.

The legal anthropologists' prejudice against Anglo-American law has no real empirical base. They perpetuate the mistaken

1. H. I. Hogbin, *Law and Order in Polynesia*, London, 1934; I. Schapera, *A Handbook of Tswana Law and Custom*, London, 1955.
2. L. Nader, "The Anthropological Study of Law" in *The Ethnography of Law, American Anthropologist*, Special Publication, L. Nader (ed.), 1965,
3. A. E. Hoebel, *The Law of Primitive Man*, New York 1968; L. Pospisil, *Kapaukau Papuans and Their Law*, New Haven, 1958.

idea that comparative work must always compare two or more
other societies. Why not 'us' and 'them'? [4] Legal anthropology
could not meet this kind of challenge because too little is known
about 'our' law. None of the anthropological definitions of law
are, in fact, genuinely universal. The attempt by anthropologists
to define 'law' or universal characteristics of law has its correla-
tive: "The very attempt of economic analysis to build a theory of
universal validity, to avoid any and all psychological commit-
ments takes it into the path of operational meaninglessness." [5]
Karl Llewellyn recognized this definitional trap and strongly advised Hoebel against attempting a definition of law.[6] Hoebel
went ahead. I deal with his attempt later. The cooperation between Llewellyn and Hoebel was in the classic interdisciplinary
tradition: Llewellyn knew little anthropology and Hoebel knew
little law.[7]

The word "jurisprudence' has conflicting meanings in the anthropological literature. At times the term is employed to refer
to a philosophy or theory of law, or an analytical scheme:
though there are occasions when it is used loosely to refer to the
'nuts and bolts' of law. Anthropologists often point out that
Western legal experience is inapplicable to primitive law systems or that its imposition may distort data.[8] If a jurist dealing
with Western law, with no training in anthropology, makes a
statement which is not appropriate to the circumstances of sim-
pler societies, then sometimes all his work tends to get dismissed
by legal anthropologists.[9] But legal anthropologists have not
paid careful attention to the kinds of juridical thinking that
might be cross-culturally applicable. In other words, the legal
anthropologists, after the fashion of Herskovits's criticism of the

4. See M. Gluckman, *Politics, Law and Ritual in Tribal Society*, Chicago,
1965, p. 209.
5. M. J. Herskovits (ed.), *Economic Anthropology*, New York, 1965, p. 45,
quoting G. Papandreou.
6. W. Twining, "The Works of Karl Llewellyn," *The Modern Law Review*,
xxxi, March 1968.
7. *Ibid*.
8. Nader, "The Anthropological Study of Law;" P. Bohannan, *Justice and
Judgment Among the Tiv*, London, 1957, p. 70.
9. Hoebel, *The Law of Primitive Man*, New York, 1968, pp. 18–28; Pospisil,
Kapaukau.

economist Marshall, have criticized lawyers who had made no real attempt to apply their findings cross-culturally.[10] Why should economic anthropology draw on the work of economists and legal anthropology ignore, or virtually do so, Anglo-American law?

Hoebel and Pospisil [11] imply that their universal definitions of law are an advance on what Western jurists have written. It is time their work was put in legal perspective because legal anthropologists seem to live in a world of their own. How do these definitions really stack up against the lawyers' own efforts? Bodin and Hobbes both believed force was an essential component of law. They did not distinguish law as a methodological postulate, an analytical device, apart from actual events. Austin appreciated the idea of sovereignty as an analytical construct; a series of assumptions linked his concepts together.[12] His scheme was at times confused since he located sovereignty in different places; he assumed the habitual obedience of men. Kelsen succeeded in theory in separating the normative and actual orders, putting forward his 'basic legal norm,' a method of achieving their reconciliation. He stressed that law be viewed as a holistic construct.

In Kelsen's theory, force is the prerogative of the collectivity rather than discrete individuals. His normative proposition was, *if* the law were broken, sanctions *ought* to be applied. Authority, wherever located in society, had the right to apply force. Legal events are systematized as a consequence of their having this 'ought to' aspect; this fiction is simply an analytical device for introducing order into a class of events. The scheme has no influence on actual events, and although it must ultimately exhibit a relationship with what actually happens, its validity is not destroyed if, after a law is broken, force is not always applied. Kelsen can claim creation of a unified analytical system; unified because the events all share this 'ought to' quality. It is

10. Herskovits, *Economic Anthropology*, pp. 509–510.
11. Hoebel, *The Law of Primitive Man*, pp. 18–28; Pospisil, *Kapaukau*.
12. J. Austin, *The Province of Jurisprudence Determined and the Uses of the Study of Jurisprudence*, London, 1954; G. Campbell, *An Analysis of Austin's Lectures on Jurisprudence*, 1917.

an intellectual framework he creates for viewing actual events. Kelsen reconciles the ideal and the actual orders with his 'basic legal norm.' Legality, or the norm, means the transformation of power (or authority) into the law.[13]

This is a more sophisticated position than that of Hoebel who makes the threat or actual application of force the ultimate test of law.[14] Hoebel denies or neglects the legal nature of psychological sanctions or the existence of administrative and international law.[15] Worse still, his scheme can be held void for uncertainty, i.e., he does not really spell out the implications of infraction being, as he says, "regularly met, etc." What constitutes regularity? This would have to be spelled out in detail, and it is quite clear that Hoebel was unable to do this with any precision. Compare for example the rather wooly *description* of regularity in Llewellyn and Hoebel [16] with Hoebel's later bare assertion of regularity without further explanation.[17] What Hoebel gives is simply an 'ideal type' in the Weberian sense of the term, i.e., it is not to be found in empirical reality. However, as I show below, it is not even a very good or accurate or useful ideal type. Weber at least regarded the individual as the only true bearer of meaning. Hoebel and other legal anthropologists ignored this notion. Nor would Weber have committed the error Hoebel has of attempting to find an ideal type in empirical reality.

Pospisil's universalist definition is also similar to Kelsen's model. Pospisil, unlike Hoebel, spells out the consequences of viewing law in terms of the opposition of ideal and actual orders. Pospisil's suggestion that law consists of "principles abstracted from the decisions of authorities," [18]—though during his

13. H. Kelsen, *General Theory of Law and State*, trans. A Wedberg, New York, 1961, pp. 405, 406, 437.

14. Hoebel, "Three Studies," p. 28.

15. See Schwarzenburger in R.H. Code-Holland and G. Schwarzenburger, *Law, Justice and Equity*, London, 1967, pp. 168–175.

16. K. N. Llewellyn and E. A. Hoebel, *The Cheyenne Way*, Norman, Okla., 1941, pp. 286–289.

17. *The Law of Primitive Man*, p. 28.

18. Pospisil, "Law and Order," in *Introduction to Cultural Anthropology*, J. A. Clifton (ed.), Boston, 1968.

Kapaukau analysis he was not able to demonstrate any such thing even allowing for dissonance between the ideal and the actual—and Hoebel's idea that systematic use of force is always present, raise a fundamental objection against 'universalism.' That is, that unlike Kelsen, neither Hoebel nor Pospisil nor Bohannan succeed in doing anything other than *implying* the existence of a legal *system*. As Hugh Duncan says: "Acts are 'integrated,' their patterns 'maintained,' or their structures 'organized,' but when we examine closely how this organization occurs we soon discover integration is assumed not demonstrated." [19] There are too many 'irregular' exceptions to the definitions to give them any real heuristic power or any claim to *systematic* behavior. Pospisil terms law as something to do with principles. He was not able to specify *exactly* or even systematically what these principles would be in particular cases. Pospisil does not acknowledge the fact but this view or definition of law had already been offered by Pound and other jurists.[20] A substantial portion of the book is given over to Pospisil's complaint that people have not followed principles.[21]

The definitional approach is not only bad law it is also bad anthropology. 'Universal' definitions of law—even Kelsen's—all somehow imply that law as a phenomenon is neither time-bound nor culture-bound . . . "The cultural goals of the group, the social history and personalities of its members, and the relationships between them—the group's cultural content—is not something to be 'added' in to any analytical scheme *post hoc*, but is intrinsic to it . . . hence the march for universalistic propositions is ultimately unproductive." [22]

Law need not be studied as an aspect of society, nor need the concerns of the lawyer and the anthropologist be thought irreconcilable. Law can only be appreciated in relation to the wider social context. It is society that controls law and not the reverse

19. H. Duncan, *Symbols in Society*, New York, 1968, p. 4.
20. See, for example, J. M. Derrett, *Introduction to Modern Hindu Law*, Bombay, 1963, pp. 7–9.
21. See, for example, pp. 161, 162.
22. P. Worsley, "Bureaucracy and Decolonization," *The New Sociology*, I. L. Horowitz (ed.), New York, 1964. This, incidentally, is a rather odd comment for one who wrote *The Trumpet Shall Sound* (1957).

as is often suggested. Where public opinion changes and new attitudes come into being we see a change in the operation of law. Authorities responsible for prosecution may no longer be willing to prosecute; those who try such offenses may grant discharges where it is within their prerogative or use judicial discretion to shield the accused from the full rigor of the law. There seem to me to be a number of similarities between 'their' legal system and 'ours' which suggest that Anglo-American concepts might be useful in analysis. The courts in most societies take some account of the character of the accused, the existence of 'mitigating circumstances'; and they look for *mens rea* (the guilty mind) in many criminal cases. Cardozo pointed to the fact that judicial decisions are at the same time acts of cultural recognition: "He (the judge) must balance all his ingredients, his philosophy, his logic, his analogies, his history, his customs, his sense of right, and all the rest, and adding a little here and taking out a little there, must determine, as wisely as he can, which weight shall tip the scales." [23] Much of the conceptual difficulty involved with 'law' stems from failure to stress sufficiently that social change is involved.[24] The change theories of the lawyer are no more satisfactory than those of the anthropologist. What the courts will in fact do is impossible to predict with precision. Law is an anthropological discipline where the existence of rules and procedures might seem to provide a sufficiently limited number of variables so as to make the legal future more certain. If for 'law' we read 'culture,' perspective is restored.[25]

Other more serious methodological criticisms of a purely anthropological nature can be made of universalist definitions of law. Two sets of books are kept. One set deals with 'jurisprudence,' talks about 'force,' 'threat,' 'authority,' 'regularity,' 'reciprocal relations,' 'conflict resolution,' 'principles,' and other con-

23. B. N. Cardozo, *The Nature of the Judicial Process*, New Haven, 1922, p. 162; M. Gluckman, *The Judicial Process Among the Barotse of Northern Rhodesia*, Manchester, 1955, pp. 363, 364.
24. See Gluckman, *ibid.*, p. 366.
25. See Code-Holland and Schwarzenburger, *Law, Justice, and Equity*, pp. 102–115, on the attempt by colonial judges to recognize indigenous cultural principles.

stituent elements that have been defined as 'law.' The precise nature of the relationships between the variables in any particular scheme is never specified. The notion of law used in relation to, or derived from, these concepts is never more than a tentative or provisional assumption that must be empirically demonstrated to be held valid. It never is. When anthropologists understand 'law' in terms of its being essentially concerned with authority and conflict resolution, then a criticism leveled against Durkheim is appropriate enough. "The meanings . . . must be those constructed by the actors involved in their 'natural cultural habitat' rather than those constructed by the actors in response to some 'unnatural' instrument with its own implicit assumptions about the structure of meanings being studied." [26] It would, perhaps, be more true to say that such theorizing would be useful if it could ultimately make events and situations more meaningful for the actors involved. There must be, at some stage, congruence between social science and real life explanations.

This is an important point because most monographs give an account of a presumed legal situation rather than a description and analysis of social reality as it is perceived by the actors involved in the situation. When Bohannan [27] maintains that law must be distinguished from custom, and then proceeds to do this with his notion of 'double institutionalization' and differing 'realms,' we have a more subtle form of 'universalism.' We have a method which does not recognize the correct use of legal concepts: lawyers believe that the language of the layman and the jurist should mean the same thing.[28] "Law is special"; it is "out of phase with society"; "law must either grow to fit the custom or it must actively reject it"; "unicentric legal systems are empowered to reach and enforce decisions"; "biocentric systems must reach legal compromises that are sufficiently compatible with both cultures as to be acceptable and ultimately enforcea-

26. J. D. Douglas, *The Social Meanings of Suicide,* Princeton, N.J., 1967, pp. 253–254.
27. P. Bohannan, "The Differing Realms of Law," *American Anthropologist,* Special Publication, L. Nader (ed.), 1965.
28. A. W. B. Simpson, "The Analysis of Legal Concepts," *Law Quarterly Review,* lxxx (1964).

ble from the two power centers." The definitional problem fi-
nally leads to this tortured distinction: "Customs are norms or
rules . . . about the ways in which people must behave if society is to endure." "Some customs are reinstitutionalized at another level: they are restated for more precise purposes of legal
institutions." Bohannan assumes that law is about social control,
but then goes on to say that one form of social control is legal,
the other nonlegal.

A kinship system 'invented' by the anthropologist tells us
something about the ways in which people actually order this
experience, it encapsulates the meanings that certain forms of
social organization have for the people concerned. But where is
the society where people organize their experience in the manner suggested by Bohannan? He does not sufficiently stress that
this model is an ideal type which will never be found in reality.
Legal concepts are not to be divorced from social reality. Legal
activity is social activity. Instead of analyzing the social meanings of the situation Bohannan has himself invested legal concepts with meaning and as a result of this he attempts to 'make
sense of the situation.' A basic defect with this kind of theorizing is that it yields a universal social science meaning rather
than a particular cultural meaning. The universal should be constructed from particulars rather than, as is too often the case
at present, particulars being 'explained' by the universal. Ideal
type legal models compounded of typical traits ought not to be
confused with ethnographic models constructed on a basis of
common or average characteristics.

The other set of books deals with cases of 'procedure' at the
expense of social reality. It involves an attempt to derive anthropological information from a *legal* analysis alone. "Cases are of
course themselves no substitute for sound theory; *but they are
the writer's and the reader's only means of checking on the theorizing*" (my emphasis).[29] Theory means "thinking thus, in nicer
terms *because the terms themselves are not ambiguous*" (my emphasis).[30]

29. Hoebel, *The Law of Primitive Man*, p. 45.
30. *Ibid.*, p. 63, quoting Llewellyn.

A possible criticism of the trouble case technique is that it is 'anec-dotal,' in the sense that crises are often not typical of ordinary life and that the cases selected for intensive analysis may well be untypical even of crisis. By concentrating on the unusual a writer may give a distorted picture of the culture he is studying. This is especially likely if the epoch-making case is preferred to the 'petty rows, the routine law-stuff.' Furthermore, if each case is to be analyzed in detail and depth, only a relatively small sample is likely to be used, with a corre-sponding decrease in the chance of its being representative. These would be valid criticisms of a work which relied on this method to the exclusion of all others. [31]

An attempt to undertake a purely legal analysis as opposed to the more broadly based inquiry of the anthropologist carries with it great dangers and cannot be expected to yield the same kinds of information. What such approaches amount to—and this applies particularly to Pospisil as well as Hoebel's use of the case method—

is the use of [cases] to illustrate general points and the use of general points to illustrate cases. The general points are neither tested nor made specific. They are adapted to the [cases], as the arrangement of the [cases] is adapted to them . . . These logical tricks are used to give apparent structural, and historical, and psychological meaning to studies which by their very style of abstraction have eliminated such meaning.

Concentration on the case method or on 'principles' has been at the expense of appreciating the individual subjective mean-ings.[32]

Why should Hoebel commend Hohfeld's scheme and yet fail to use it consistently himself? [33] In fact he uses Hohfeld to ex-plain the cases in the earlier part of his book and then uses the cases to explain the law later on after the fashion of Mill's 'ab-stracted empiricism.' "Hohfeld's analysis makes ['laws'] unambig-uously clear. Hohfeld's fundamental concepts fit not only the fundamental legal relations, *but also the fundamentals of any*

31. Twining, "Karl Llewellyn."
32. C. Wright Mills, *The Sociological Imagination*, New York, 1959. Gluckman, *Politics, Law and Ritual*, pp. 191–193.
33. Hoebel, *The Law of Primitive Man*.

complex of normative or imperative social reciprocity" (my emphasis).[34] In other words the Hohfeld scheme cannot indicate what law is. The model is an 'ideal type' and not always an accurate one at that when one turns to analysis of 'typical' legal relations, even in Western societies.[35] Hoebel's 'abstracted empiricism' is quite obvious. For the first part of the book (pp. 67–126), principles are used to illustrate the cases; in the middle portion (pp. 126–210), cases are used to produce principles; then in the final section dealing with Ashanti law, Hoebel reverts to using principles to illustrate cases. Little attention is paid to the wider context, the subjective meanings as they ramify through the total beliefs and values of the various societies. The result is an analysis of an 'ideal type' divorced from society reality. And Hoebel, beyond his bare assertions of what 'law' is, is unable to illustrate the validity of his definition in a real life situation.

Pospisil's study of the Kapaukau aims to "demonstrate with the help of Papuan data the effectiveness of a theory of law formulated on the basis of a comparative study of thirty-two cultures and a survey of an additional sixty-three." [36] It is an even more classic case of 'abstracted empiricism' than Hoebel's analysis. Why Pospisil's theory could not have stood on its own after such impressive preconditioning, and why it needed the Kapaukau study, is a mystery. It is one thing to accept an ethnographer's account of what he believes has happened in the field supported by data one can examine, but it is surely a totally different matter to accept opinion multiplied thirty-two times without any evidence at all. Under these rules there is nothing to prevent me from saying that I have undertaken a cross-cultural comparison of one hundred societies and a survey of an additional sixty-nine and I find Pospisil wrong. His theorizing is very weak and it is rather surprising that his conclusions have not been challenged before.

Pospisil's analysis of legal cases shows how specific knowledge of Anglo-American law might be useful. "One may still defend an exclusive study of the rules by pointing out that the devia-

34. *Ibid.*, p. 63.
35. R. W. M. Dias, *Jurisprudence*, London, 1964, pp. 226–249.
36. Pospisil, "Law and Order," p. 3.

tions in the results are due to aggravating as well as alleviating circumstances and to situations not defined in the rules. The rest of the cases which do not reflect corresponding rules may be labelled as showing injustice on the part of authority." [37] Pospisil completely ignores the subjective individual meanings of the situation and he orders the data without any discernible rules. The cases which Pospisil uses to support this assertion all involve 'authority' in the shape of a chief or headman as defendant (save one, where the data he gives is completely inconclusive).[38] What we see in fact, if we wish to see whether Anglo-American law could be useful, is an inability to take legal action in tort against authority. This position is no different in law from the state of affairs in England prior to 1947. Prior to enactment of the Crown Proceedings Act of 1947 in England, a subject could not sue the Crown in tort, save in cases where the Crown gave permission for the suit.[39] This is a matter of political expediency, the same kind of expediency that gives diplomats immunity during their public service.[40]

Or take Pospisil's case no. 25.[41] In this case a young man seized the breasts of an unmarried girl, an offense which warranted a fine of 2Km. The authority, amused by the youth's clumsy attempt to seduce the girl, paid the fine himself, and then advised the boy on the arts of seduction. Pospisil says rather stiffly "the authority's action is not just." [42] In English law a man might bring and win a case under the strict letter of the relevant act or statute. The spirit behind the law asserts itself through the awarding of 'contemptuous damages.' Such damages acknowledge that the case has been won but emphasize that the case ought never to have been brought to court.[43] The headman in this case obeys the letter of the law but he shows by his treat-

37. *Ibid.*, p. 251.
38. *Ibid.*, pp. 139–143.
39. R. F. V. Heuston (ed.), *Salmond on the Law of Torts*, London, 1965, pp. 63–67.
40. See also M. Barkun, *Law Without Sanctions*, New Haven, 1968, on law without sanctions.
41. Pospisil, "Law and Order," pp. 161, 162.
42. *Ibid.*
43. Heuston, *Law of Torts*, p. 734.

ment of the boy that the case ought never to have been brought in the first place.

Pospisil's attributes of law—authority, universal application, obligation, sanction—when applied to Kapaukau data lead him to suggest that 44 out of 126 cases were nonlegal.[44] But the Kapaukau cannot say what Pospisil's 'legality' means to them, if anything at all. All notions of social reality have been subordinated to the quest for a universal definition. Llewellyn was more sensitive to the needs of anthropology than Pospisil.[45] Too much time and effort has been wasted on the search for this Holy Grail. Pospisil unwittingly attempted the impossible: he like Hoebel attempted to find an ideal type in empirical reality.

Bohannan says: "One of the best ways to perceive . . . 'laws' is to break up the law into smaller components, capable of attaching to persons . . . and so to work in terms of rights and duties. The relationships between law and custom, law and morals, law and anything else can be seen in a new light. In fact, if it is not carried too far . . ."[46] The last is a major point. Can Hohfeld's analysis be distinguished from the position of the Malinowskian "reciprocalists"[47] or made to work in an unencyclopedic way other than by illegitimately and intuitively, *prejudging* what constitutes law? It is only if one *knows* what constitutes law that Hohfeld's schemes can be made to have any use at all. And too few legal anthropologists have appreciated that Hohfeld's scheme is another ideal type which may not be found in reality.[48] And, as I have said, anthropologists who have used the universalist approach have never really *proved* what law is. In fact, each universalist disagrees with the theory of everybody else.

A major irony is that the anthropological critics of Western jurisprudence have transplanted most of its supposed attributes

44. Pospisil, "Law and Order," pp. 257, 272.
45. Twining, "Karl Llewellyn."
46. Bohannan, "The Differing Realms of Law."
47. B. Malinowski, "Introduction to H. I. Hogbin," *Law and Order in Polynesia*, 1934.
48. On 'ideal types,' see Douglas, *Social Meanings of Suicide*, p. 237, and R. Aron, *Main Currents in Sociological Thought*, vol. II, New York, 1970, pp. 244–270.

—in disassociated and haphazard form admittedly—such as force, certainty, and conflict, without being aware of their own ethnocentrism. When Nader mentioned the familiar chapters on contracts, torts, etc., she overlooked the fact that, as far as I can see, no anthropologists except Gluckman have ever made use of the standard works of Western lawyers devoted to contracts, torts, etc., in our society. Gluckman believes "the very refinement of English Jurisprudence makes it a better instrument for analysis." He says that "gaps exist because I did not think of the problems when I was working among the Barotse and hence did not collect the information I might have. If I point out these gaps other anthropologists may collect the appropriate data." [49]

He has not followed this refinement consistently for example in his treatment of contract.[50] He uses contract in the broad sense that most legal anthropologists do, something that is little more than agreement. Yet it would surely be an advantage for anthropologists to look for the ingredients our own courts look for. A lawyer looking at contract would ask what the constituent elements are. Offer: how must this be made? Acceptance: how must this be signified? Capacity to enter into legal relations: have the parties to the contract the legal ability to enter into an agreement? Consideration: must both parties receive something of value? *Consensus ad idem:* are both parties really in agreement about the subject matter of the contract? [51] The aim is clarity, and anthropologists could well have found out a great deal by asking such questions without fear of distortion. The same might be said of other branches of Western law which legal anthropologists have ignored.

Other examples of what one might term 'middle range' theories are the lawyer's analytical concepts of *mens rea*, the guilty mind, and *actus reus*, the action. Lawyers distinguish between mental states and *mens rea* [52] and try to use *mens rea* and *actus*

49. Gluckman, *Politics, Law and Ritual*, pp. xiv, sv.
50. *Ibid.*, pp. 171–203.
51. Sir William Anson, *Principles of the English Law of Contract*, Oxford, 1964, shows, with interesting examples, how these elements are looked for in the English law of contract.
52. J. W. G. Turner (ed.), *Kennys Outlines of Criminal Law*, Cambridge, 1966.

reus together. It is this point which makes the analysis of the jurist similar to that of the anthropologist: the jurist does not dwell exclusively on *mens rea* or *actus reus;* like the anthropologist, he views legal acts holistically. This ties in with a comment I made earlier that if anthropologists use terms which have precise and special meanings for lawyers then they must employ them correctly.[53]

Legal anthropology will only progress to the extent that anthropologists make a serious attempt to explore systematically what ought to have been in the minds of the anthropologists who wrote the 'familiar chapters.' They must study our law, experience its discipline, the ways it has changed, how it is made, and altered. There is no need for distortion if one uses Anglo-American legal concepts any more than is the case with economic anthropologists who use concepts derived from Western experience. It would be more easy to accept the substantivist position if one had more confidence that it had a satisfactory empirical base.

Bohannan begins *Justice and Judgment Among the Tiv* by stating: "I am not trained in law . . . my knowledge of law and my reading in it are extremely limited" (p.v). Later he says: "Needless to say, our categories of contract and of tort are not coterminous with the Tiv category of debt" (p. 112). Now what evidence is there for this assertion about our categories of tort and contract? His statement in *Social Anthropology* [54] that "law is one of the best studied subdisciplines of anthropology; the literature is small but of high quality," would be more convincing if he had shown a greater appreciation of Anglo-American law. To anyone with legal training it is a statement of most doubtful validity.

But, have not the works of legal anthropologists been most favorably reviewed in learned law journals? Yes. But, one finds, most amusingly, that the reviewers were *other* sociologists and anthropologists.[55] Obviously, lawyers took one look and saw

53. *Ibid.*, pp. 17–56.
54. New York, 1963, p. 284.
55. See, for example, the reviewers mentioned on the cover of Hoebel, *The Law of Primitive Man.*

something very alien to their own concerns and ways of think-ing. It is obvious—one needs only examine bibliographies—that many of those anthropologists who have talked authoritatively about law using terms like contract and tort, have never con-sulted our own law in anything other than a superficial way.

This is an area where one might have expected the work of applied anthropologists to have exercised a beneficial influence on the general research scene. Certainly there is much that ought to have attracted the attention of applied workers. The reason that things were not different is, for Foster,[56] one of the strengths of applied work, though to my mind, a major weak-ness; that is, that all anthropologists have had the same training. The results are not very spectacular, and there is an obvious need for a greater degree of cooperation between lawyers and anthropologists concerned with the modernization process. I suggest that academic legal anthropology has few useful insights for those entrusted with the creation of legislation thought ap-propriate in the context of modernization.[57]

Legislative measures enacted in pursuit of the goals of mod-ernization may be designed to promote or sustain change.[58] Anthropological studies of native courts or traditional forms of land tenure, for instance, have had a predominantly conserva-tive or historical focus. They have in the main been concerned more with the past and the present than the future. It has not been easy for the anthropologist to reconcile what he knows about law as the people see it with what he hears about law as a government would like to see it.[59] There may be several dis-tinct ethnic groups in the country or marked antagonism be-tween the peoples of different regions. All this must mean that the advice of the average anthropologist would be of limited value in legislating for a whole country because very few an-thropologists have experience of a whole country or more than

56. G. M. Foster, *Applied Anthropology*, Boston, 1969, p. 45.
57. See Gluckman, *Politics, Law and Ritual*, p. 169.
58. Sir Ivor William Jennings, *The Approach to Self-Government*, Cam-bridge, 1956.
59. See Bohannan, "The Differing Realms of Law." A very similar though more carefully worked out view is W. B. Harvey, *Law and Social Change in Ghana*, Princeton, N. J., 1966, pp. 239–271.

one ethnic group. But would anthropological advice, even for
his own group area, be of much importance to policymakers and
legislators?

When a government moves to institute 'democratic procedures,' 'income tax provisions,' a homicide act, or even local
government bylaws, there comes a time when officials have to
decide what form the legislation is to take—what kinds of safe-
guard must be made, what deterrents are deemed to be necessary, must permissions be given, what exceptions can be made.
How does one give legal expression to an administrative or political wish? It is not easy. The document must pay careful attention to existing rights and obligations of individuals and
groups; it must not infringe on other existing legislation or clash
with traditional religious customs; it must be open to minute
scrutiny by the highest court in the land; it must be the kind of
legislation that the authorities can enforce; it must be simple
enough to be understood by those at whom it is directed as well
as by those responsible for its enforcement. All this rests on a
presupposition that certain facts do exist, and that people, given
the enactment of the new legislation, will be likely to respond in
a certain fashion. Few governments like to enact legislation unless they have to—the process is usually long, tedious, and cum-
bersome.

Constitutional lawyers and other legal draftsmen have an eye
to the practical task: the number of clauses; the saving clauses;
whether the proposed legislation conflicts with some international or constitutional obligation; whether the language is perhaps too vague and ambiguous, thus encouraging noncompli-
ance or excessive litigation; whether, if circumstances change,
extensive revision will be necessary; and so on. These are very
technical concerns, and it is not unnatural that draftsmen like to
see how other countries with similar problems have attempted
the same task. There is also the added, and attractive, advantage that the experience of other countries in terms of cases,
won or lost, and objections raised, can further help the draftsmen. Therefore, draftsmen, once they have received drafting instructions from the executive, will often abstract from the legislation of other countries whole acts, statutes, or ordinances.

Often only minor changes in legislative measures enacted by other countries are required before the measure is presented to the local legislative body for approval. The language of the lawyer is at times fairly universal, and so it may be that the explanation for that particular piece of legislation which the executive tacks on (called Objects & Reasons) may be the only thing which really distinguishes it from the legislation of another country. This was particularly true of British colonial legislation. However, the whole process, though it sounds fairly straightforward, does require extensive research and considerable skill. I might here add that, surprisingly, those responsible for the drafting of the constitutional provisions of former British colonies have never heard an anthropologist express the remotest concern with what they were doing.

Constitutional lawyers in turn have paid little attention to the importance of cultural variation [60] and so we find, for example, that the constitutions of India and Pakistan are not very much different from that of the Republic of Ireland.[61] There is clearly a need for the introduction of an anthropological dimension which must await the time when anthropologists establish more effective cooperation with constitutional lawyers. At present no anthropologists are trained for this work, and none are being trained to the best of my knowledge.

The executive is most concerned with whether the drafting instructions, which eventually give rise to the legislation at the hands of the legal draftsmen, are an adequate statement of public intent. There must be some assessment by officials of probable reaction by members of the public. This is where the administrator relies on the experience of his own officers in the field, and also of a wide range of individuals and associations.[62] No government, no matter how keen on the achievement of goals, wishes to enact legislation which might lead to widespread pub-

60. O. Hood Philips, "The Making of a Colonial Constitution," F1, *Law Quarterly Review*, 1955; S. A. DeSmith. "Mauritius: Constitution in a Plural Society," *Modern Law Review*, XXXI (1968).
61. Jennings, *The Law and the Constitution*, London, 1963, gives details of constitutional provisions in these countries in the appendices to his book.
62. See Lord Hailey, "Introduction to C. K. Meek," *Land, Law and Custom in the Colonies*, London, 1949.

lic disobedience or disaffection. Even if measures are accurately forecast as being unpopular, and yet are felt necessary for the national good, they must nevertheless be looked at in terms of the likelihood of the government being able to provide adequate resources for reinforcement.

The anthropologist could not replace, or take over, the functions either of the draftsman or the executive. Neither could he assume over-all responsibility. The trouble is that anthropologists, though they may know a great deal about the law of their people, do not know enough about what *might* be done, or what *can* be done to promote the goals of modernization through legislative activity. Though the anthropologist talks about land tenure, for example, it is not surprising that most of the studies on land tenure have been done by men with administrative experience.[63] So the anthropologist is often not in a position to recommend how the issues should be tackled because he does not know any, or nearly enough about, nonnative land law. He has not made himself familiar with what has been done in similar cases in other parts of the world. He is usually quite satisfied to rely on what *other anthropologists* have written. The thing that many anthropologists clamor for government authorities to recognize, their right and 'fittedness' to give advice on policy formation, is the one thing that they are usually least qualified to demand. What was, and what is, are really very different from what might be. The anthropologist is perhaps less well qualified to offer advice on the kinds of legislation required than a member of the community he is studying, because all too frequently he does not have a very clear idea of what their legal system really is, as *they* see it.

This is the weakest area in the anthropology of development. It is a sad state of affairs which will take years to rectify, years of waiting, while anthropologists acquire necessary legal skills and become more sensitive to the concerns of lawyers. The ethnography of law appears to have proceeded on the assumption that anthropologists were doing quite a satisfactory job if they

63. Cf. C. K. Meek, *Law and Authority in a Nigerian Tribe,* London, 1937; C. H. Allen, *Customary Land Tenure in the British Solomon Islands Protectorate,* Honiara, 1959.

could appreciate the universal meaning of law. To a lesser extent they worried about what 'law' actually meant to the people themselves. There was no felt need to turn to Anglo-American law for inspiration.

I am suggesting that for practical and academic purposes legal anthropology could benefit from the example provided by the revolution in economic anthropology. Economic anthropologists have not had to become economists in order to derive benefits from Western experience. My conclusion is that a careful analysis of Anglo-American law could provide a number of useful ideas and concepts. At present legal anthropology is neither sound law nor sound anthropology; had applied anthropology not been subordinated to academic criteria and objectives then there probably would have been effective liaison between lawyers and anthropologists. Another victim of community schemes! The major problem of the moment is to justify the title 'legal anthropology.' Little progress will be made by anthropologists so long as they continue to attempt to undertake legal analysis using anthropological insights. Progress can be made by applying ordinary or traditional anthropology aided by the insights gained from what I have termed 'middle range' legal theory. We should spend more time trying to define social reality and less time trying to define law.

X

Conclusions

Applied anthropology has mainly been concerned with small-scale community development schemes. Development ought, for anthropologists, to involve more than this—nonanthropologists can perform pretty well anyway—and some areas so far totally neglected by applied anthropology must now be tackled.

The potential role of the development anthropologist can be broken down into three components. The first is concerned with a knowledge of the culture of the people one attempts to work with. Problems to be solved here include that of the time required to obtain data, in view of the slowness of traditional fieldwork, and that of the need to develop statements of broad application, in view of the traditional focus on community studies. The second component is concerned with knowledge of development work, in particular the contributions by other disciplines and professions. Here the problem has been that the lack of suitable training and experience has put the anthropologist in the position of a layman. Though the anthropologist could, from his cultural data, determine broadly the popularity or unpopularity of measures, a knowledge of the history of other projects, the 'nuts and bolts' of applied work, requires a knowledge or experience of organizational delivery systems. Academics have to appreciate the practicalities of administration, they have to assess the extent to which the written word can produce positive benefits on the ground in addition to those normally associated with the dissemination of knowledge. This is the third component.

What does matter is what is done, as well as what is written, and the fact that social scientists and authorities work together. There may be overlapping of fields of specialization—and there ought to be—but each social scientist or professional has the ability to do something in depth, a particular kind of competence that his colleagues do not share. However, until anthropologists pay more attention to the needs, capacities, and specialties of other people on the development scene they will continue to have a limited utility. The anthropology of development will never get anywhere on a part-time basis. This is the unfortunate state of affairs at present.

Yet, it would be impossible for me to answer in detail the question: "What will development anthropologists actually do?" They will 'do' anthropology, fill in forms and obey regulations, activities not unknown in university life. Before the question can be answered in greater detail a great deal must happen. Let me recapitulate something of what I said about the two types of development anthropologist, the academic and the general practitioner.

Academic anthropologists will have to broaden their knowledge and then specialize in, say, economic or legal anthropology if they wish to maximize their potential. Apart from personal inclination this must be the case if general practitioners are to receive adequate university training. Some academic anthropologists will wish to work on problems of their own choosing but there must be a greater willingness to work on problems formulated by authorities. If the academic anthropologists have had suitable training and if they work in conjunction with other social scientists then other fruitful lines of inquiry may present themselves. These can be put to the authorities.

The general practitioners I see as people who have obtained broad or specialized competence in anthropology but who do not wish to pursue a university career. It is necessary for these people to develop skills to function as members of what I term a development team in the field. Some may do staff work. Theirs is the task of supplying an anthropological dimension in the day to day activities of international agencies and governments. To cover the kinds of training required I have coined the awkward phrase 'nonspecialized specialization.' In this profession I see personal characteristics as being of the greatest importance.

Governments and agencies must be informed more about what anthropology *can* do. They can then assess what kinds of positions might be created to fulfill their objectives. However, professional associations must do a little more than they have done in the past to represent anthropology in international forums. It seems more than reasonable to emphasize the potential contribution that could be made by economic, political, legal, medical, or even general anthropologists. Planning is failing to achieve its purpose in countries whose citizens want change, and international agency development is becoming more and more bureaucratic. It makes sense to recruit the help of anthropology.

But it would not have made very good sense for authorities to have enthusiastically embraced applied anthropology. They did not. The problem of our public image is still with us. Anthropologists are still thought of as individualistic, withdrawn, odd people, who delight in strange languages and customs. Their knowledge is usually more of the 'would-you-believe-it' than the 'now-we-know-we-can-get-ahead' variety. We need to give talks and lectures to the staffs of international agencies and governments. Anthropology should be taught during their training programs. Even though other social scientists may be aware of the potential utility of anthropology, not until the same facts are appreciated by administrators will there be a significant change. Someone accuses me of making a plea for jobs for anthropologists? Yes, that is exactly what I am doing. It should have been done a long time ago. But I make no plea for applied anthropology.

Anthropologists, however, cannot succumb to the temptation of passing final judgment on all plans. Imagination is needed to assess the over-all implications of what is proposed; tolerance is required to accept the plans of *other* professionals and social scientists. As I said, it is only a short passage—unfortunately taken by too many applied anthropologists in the past—from believing one knows a lot about a people to believing one knows what is best for them. Applied anthropology was heir to colonial paternalism.

It is no more easy to lay down an ethical code than it is to say in any great detail what kind of anthropology must be followed. However, some comfort can be taken from the fact that there never has been an ethics of result, only of intention. We have to look very closely at our own intentions. We have to be quite sure that all the facts have been taken into account, that we carefully assess the benefits against the costs. There will be a price for this kind of work. For the anthropologist it may be an uneasy conscience; for those he aids it may be frustration or unhappiness. Academic dissemination of information can do a great deal when minds in daily contact with the pressing problems of development are becoming dulled toward sensitive matters.

We might say the great failure of applied anthropology was an inability to produce a sound theory of social change. We could produce one if we accepted the applied anthropologist's definition of his role as an academic rather than a practitioner. In my view it is time to discard this definition; and I do not intend to offer any theory of social change. Indeed I caution against such attempts.

Though theorizing about social change is undeniably important, it must not be allowed to obscure the fact that we do not yet possess good social change theories, and we have to achieve results with what we know at present. Model building in anthropology has become an end rather than a means. There are cogent reasons why such enterprises can be dangerous for the development anthropologist working in the field, with responsibility for implementation of specific programs. Common sense reasons.

It is not really necessary to have a *theory* about the future, in order to do things now. Governments have functioned for a fairly long time without a social change theory that works. And this is better than having a theory that does not work. Yes, it is a worthwhile *goal*, but we live in the present! Most development plans are a compound of common sense and experience and, as I said, are pretty much trial balloons. They are not doomed because we do not know for certain what is going to happen in the future. Flexibility permits change. One gives a personal opinion, and it may be wrong. Besides, it must be borne in mind that anthropological theory may, perhaps, only *contribute* to the understanding achieved by planners; other people may have equally good ideas and theories. Applied anthropologists always wrote as if theirs were the only theories. The task can be to describe what has been and what is in terms that are understood by, and are useful to, one's colleagues who are not themselves professional anthropologists.

Anthropologists will be concerned to permit change to take place rather than trying to make it take place. They will be interested in a people's own definition of their situation. It seems plausible that people will tend to change more in conformity with the ideas they have of their own circumstances than with anthropological theory which, of course, they know nothing of. This is neglected by many anthropologists. A man says 'it's raining,' and we rush to analyze what he *really* means. This danger could be called 'theocentrism.'

Theocentrism means thinking anthropological theory can explain anything connected with modernization. It is an obvious danger where cooperation with other social scientists and professionals is required. Until we have successfully tested our change theories under a wide variety of situations and circumstances the tendency to distort must be held so great (besides the history of our attempts being so bad) that our mistaken notions cannot be allowed to become critical in the determination of future policy. Those who feel that because they are anthropologists, and 'know,' and therefore ought to control policy, are mistaken in their choice of career. Development relies heavily on common sense and judgment. Anthropologists do not have an exclusive lien on common sense or judgment.

But then neither do economists, who have almost totally dominated the planning process in developing countries. Neither do sociologists, political scientists, or constitutional lawyers. The situation is exacerbated because there is relatively little genuine interdisciplinary research by the well-known scholars in these disciplines. There is a tremendous dispersal of effort. Researchers in different disciplines in different countries work on problems that are often quite similar. Tiny learned societies and associations are formed to propagate interest in particular aspects of development. The proliferation is typically academic and it makes one despair of ever achieving an effective response from the universities to development problems. The stress is upon study, specialization, further analysis, and publication.

Let me indicate my pessimism with a personal anecdote. Recently I offered to teach, in addition to my normal load, a seminar on nonviolence. I attended a meeting with other faculty and students to work out details. Faculty were not to be paid for teaching though everyone was very keen to have academic credit for the course. I said I did not think that the question of credit was very important, that we had to educate ourselves, and then get to the community. It was my strong feeling that the university would have to come to terms with the outside world. Discussion at the meeting continued to focus on reading lists and the danger of students 'goofing-off.' Credit had to be given lest the project be confused with R.O.T.C. type activities! The whole episode reminded me of applied anthropology.

We have no time for the traditional slow response. There is a war on. Social science (and anthropology) has got to 'get-it-all-together' in a hurry. Now, as the film *South Pacific* which I mentioned earlier says, I have had my dream, will it come true?

Universities can initiate the kinds of training programs that could make use of anthropologists who do not wish to spend their lives in academia. It is to be hoped that when anthropologists are trained, progress can be made on the international front in persuading the authorities of the need to use them without their having to go through a lengthy war of attrition on paper.

Anthropologists interested in practical development work could achieve a more interesting and perhaps worthwhile perspective than that presented by applied anthropology. Anthropologists in the universities who are not afraid to become involved should demonstrate what can be done, rather than trying to use theories which have not yet been invented or successfully tested. Let us be pragmatic because that is what development is all about.

George Foster's view of development work, which is representative of applied anthropological thinking, is as follows:

Anthropologists belong to an academic and scientific discipline, characterized by the assumption that search for new knowledge represents the highest value . . . planners and administrators belong to professions normally characterized by the assumption that the achievement of organizational goals represents the highest value . . . members of the two groups have different expectations about their proper role behavior . . . in anthropology: a combination of the stimulation that comes from teaching, from discussions with colleagues, and from freedom to pick research topics, with time to carry out research and, especially important, time to write up in detail the results of scientific research. A big university, obviously, is seen by most anthropologists as most nearly the ideal environment in which to perform their role. An anthropologist working on an applied assignment certainly takes satisfaction in knowing that administrators and technical experts—his immediate colleagues—feel he is making an important contribution to program goals. But this approbation alone is not enough to keep an anthropologist happy for long. If he already has an established reputation he can afford the luxury of a summer, or even one or two years, in an applied assignment, gambling that the insights and knowledge he acquires from this experience will, in the long run, be valuable to him. A young man just starting the ladder to success must think longer. He must weigh the advantages of a rich applied experience against the likelihood that he will not have the publication record he needs for advancement if he returns to academic work. For him ability to please non-academic personnel in the action organization is satisfying, but does not lend to the most rapid progress in his chosen field.[1]

Everything I know about development work, and all I can see for anthropologists in it, is opposed to this view.

1. *Applied Anthropology,* Boston, 1969, pp. 156–160.

Bibliography

Adams, H. S., G. M. Foster, P. S. Taylor. *Report on Community Development Programs in India, Pakistan, and the Philippines.* Washington, D. C., 1955.

Adams, R. N., *et al. Social Change in Latin America Today.* New York, 1960.

Adelman, I. *Theories of Economic Growth and Development.* Stanford, 1962.

Allen, C. H. *Customary Land Tenure in the British Solomon Islands Protectorate* Honiara, 1959.

Allen, C. K. *Law in the Making,* Oxford, 1927.

American Anthropologist. Special Publication. *The Ethnography of Law.* Edited by L. Nader. 1965.

Anson, Sir William. *Principles of the English Law of Contract.* Oxford, 1964.

Arensberg, C. M., and A. H. Niehoff. *Introducing Social Change.* Chicago, 1964.

Argyle, M. V. *et al. Phipson on Evidence.* London, 1960.

Aron, R. *Main Currents in Sociological Thought,* vol. II. New York, 1970.

Austin, J. *The Province of Jurisprudence Determined and the Uses of the Study of Jurisprudence.* London, 1954.

Barkun, M. *Law Without Sanctions.* New Haven, 1968.

Barnett, H. G. Anthropology as an Applied Science. *Human Organization,* XVII, no. 1 (1958).

—— *Anthropology in Administration.* Evanston, 1956.

Barton, R. F. *Ifugao Law*. Berkeley, 1919.

Batten, T. R. *Communities and Their Development*. London, 1957.

Bauer, P. T., and B. S. Yamey. Economic Progress and Occupational Distribution. *Economic Journal*. December 1951.

Beattie, J. *Other Cultures*. New York, 1964.

Becker, H. S. Notes on the Concept of Commitment. *American Journal of Sociology*, LXVI, no. 1 (July 1960).

Bellows, R. J. An Appraisal of the Internship Program. *Personnel Administration*, II (March 1940).

Belshaw, C. S. *Island Administration in the South West Pacific*. London, 1950.

—— *Under the Ivi Tree—Society and Economic Growth in Rural Fiji*. Berkeley, 1964.

Bhagwati, J. *The Economics of Underdeveloped Countries*. New York, 1967.

Black, M., and D. Metzer. Ethnographic Description and the Study of Law. *American Anthropologist*. Special Publication. *The Ethnography of Law*, 1965.

Blanchard, W. El proyecto Peru-Cornell. *Peru Indigena*, V, no. 12 (1953).

Blank, D. M., and G. T. Stigler. *The Demand and Supply of Scientific Personnel*. New York, 1957.

Boeke, J. H. *Economics and Economic Policy of Dual Societies*. New York, 1953.

Bohannan, P. *Justice and Judgment Among the Tiv*. London, 1957.

—— *African Homicide and Suicide*. Princeton, 1960.

——*Social Anthropology*, New York, 1963.

——Anthropology and the Law. *Horizons in Anthropology*. Edited by Sol Tax. Chicago, 1964.

——The Differing Realms of Law. *American Anthropologist*. Special Publication. Edited by L. Nader. 1965.

Bruton, H. J. Growth Models and Underdeveloped Economies. *The Journal of Political Economy*. August 1955.

Bruton, H. J. *The Principles of Development Economics*. Englewood Cliffs, N.J., 1965.

Buckland, W. W. *The Main Institutions of Roman Private Law*. Cambridge, 1931.

Burling, R. Maximization Theories and the Study of Economic Anthropology. *American Anthropologist*, LXIV (1962).

Cairncross, A. K. *Factors in Economic Development*. London, 1962.

Cairne, H. *Law and the Social Sciences*. London, 1964.

Campbell, G. *An Analysis of Austin's Lectures on Jurisprudence*. 1917.

Caplow, T. *Principles of Organization.* New York, 1964.

Cardozo, B. N. *The Nature of the Judicial Process.* New Haven, 1922.

Chapple, E. D. Anthropological Engineering: Its Use to Administrators. *Applied Anthropology,* II, no. 2 (1943).

Cheshire, G. C., and C. H. Fifoot. *The Law of Contract.* London, 1964.

Cochrane, D. G. Review of J. S. G. Wilson's *Economic Survey of the New Hebrides in Economica.* May 1968.

—— The Administration of Wagina Resettlement Scheme. *Human Organization.* Summer 1970.

——*Big Men and Cargo Cults.* Oxford, 1970.

Code-Holland, R. H., and G. Schwarzenburger. *Law, Justice and Equality.* London, 1967.

Cohen, Sir Andrew. *British Policy in Changing Africa.* Evanston, 1959.

Cowen, A., and P. B. Carter. *Essays on the Law of Evidence.* Oxford, 1956.

Dalton, G. Economic Theory and Primitive Society. *American Anthropologist,* LXIII (1961).

—— Traditional Production in Primitive African Economics. *Quarterly Journal of Economics,* LXXVI, no. 3 (1962).

—— Primitive Money. *American Anthropologist,* LXVII (1965).

Dean, E. R. *The Supply Responses of African Farmers.* Amsterdam, 1966.

Derrett, J. M. *Introduction to Modern Hindu Law.* Bombay, 1963.

DeSmith, S. A. Mauritius: Constitution in a Plural Society. *Modern Law Review,* xxxi (1968).

Dias, R. W. M. *Jurisprudence.* London, 1964.

Dimock, M. E. The Administrative Staff College: Executive Development in Government and Industry. *American Political Science Review,* L (March 1956).

Dimock, M. E. et al. *Public Administration.* New York, 1960.

Doob, L. W. *Communication in Africa.* New Haven, 1961.

Douglas, J. D. *The Social Meanings of Suicide.* Princeton, 1967.

Dube, S. C. *Indian Village.* London, 1955.

Duncan, H. *Symbols in Society.* New York, 1968.

Eckause, R. E. Economic Criteria for Education and Training. *Review of Economics and Statistics,* XLV, no. 2 (May 1964).

Eicher, C., and L. Witt. *Agriculture in Economic Development.* New York, 1964.

Einzig, P. *Primitive Money.* London, 1949.

Erasmus, C. J. *Man Takes Control.* Minneapolis, 1961.

Evans-Pritchard, E. E. *Social Anthropology.* London, 1964.

Firth, R. *The Elements of Social Organization*. Boston, 1964.
—— *Man and Culture: An Evaluation of the Work of Bronislaw Malinowski*. New York, 1964.
—— and B. S. Yamey. eds. *Capital, Saving and Credit in Peasant Societies*. Chicago, 1964.
Food and Agriculture Organization. *Agricultural Commodities Projections for 1970*. Rome, 1962.
Foster, G. M. *Traditional Cultures: And the Impact of Technological Change*. New York, 1962.
—— *Applied Anthropology*. Boston, 1969.
Furse, R. *Aucuparius, Recollections of a Recruiting Officer*. London, 1962.
Galbraith, J. K. *Economic Development*. Cambridge, 1964.
Gerschenkron, A. *Economic Backwardness in Historical Perspective*. Cambridge, 1962.
Gibson, W. C., H. S. Masters, E. F. Wittee. *Report on Community Development Programs in India, Iran, Egypt, and the Gold Coast*. Washington, D. C., 1955.
Ginsburg, N. S. The Great City in Southeast Asia. *The American Journal of Sociology*, LX (1955).
Gluckman, M. *The Judicial Process Among the Barotse of Northern Rhodesia*. Manchester, 1955.
—— *Custom and Conflict in Africa*. Glencoe, 1955.
—— African Jurisprudence. *Advancement of Science*. 75:439–454 (1962).
—— *The Ideas in Barotse Jurisprudence*. New Haven, 1965.
—— *Politics, Law and Ritual in Tribal Society*. Chicago, 1965.
Goodenough, W. H. *Cooperation in Change*. New York, 1963.
Gouldner, A. W., and S. M. Miller, eds. *Applied Sociology*. New York, 1965.
Gulliver, P. H. *Social Control in an African Society*. Boston, 1963.
Gurvitch, G. D. *Sociology of Law*. New York, 1942.
Hagen, E. E. *Planning Economic Development*. Homewood, Ill., 1963.
—— *The Economics of Development*. Cambridge, 1968.
Hailey, Lord. Introduction to C. K. Meek, *Land, Law and Custom in the Colonies*. London, 1949.
Hamilton, W. B., ed. *The Transfer of Institutions*. Durham, North Carolina, 1964.
Harris, C. Decentralization. *Journal of Public Administration*, III (April 1925).
Harrison, F. *On Jurisprudence and the Conflict of Laws*. Oxford, 1919.

Harvey, W. B. *Law and Social Change in Ghana*. Princeton, 1966.

Herskovits, M. J., ed. *Economic Anthropology*. New York, 1965.

Heuston, R. F. V., ed. *Salmond on the Law of Torts*. 1965.

Hildebrand, G. H. *Growth and Structure in the Economy of Modern Italy*. Cambridge, 1965.

Hoebel, A. E. Three Studies in African Law. *Stanford Law Review*, no. 3 (1961).

―――― *The Law of Primitive Man*, New York, 1968.

Hogbin, H. I. *Law and Order in Polynesia*. London, 1934.

―――― *Social Change*. London, 1958.

Holmberg, A. R. The Research and Development Approach to the Study of Change. *Human Organization*, XVII, no. 1 (1958).

――――and M. Vasquez. Un proyecto de Antropologia aplicada en el Peru. *Revista Museo Nacional*, XX. 1958.

Hoselitz, B. F. Role of Cities in the Economic Growth of Underdeveloped Countries. *Journal of Political Economy*. June 1953.

―――― The City, the Factory, and Economic Growth. *American Economic Review*. May 1955.

―――― Non-Economic Factors in Economic Development. *American Economic Review*. May 1957.

Howell, P. P. *A Manual of Nuer Law*. London, 1954.

Jenks, E. *The Book of English Law*. 6th ed. By P. B. Fairest. Athens, Ohio, 1967.

Jennings, Sir Ivor William. *The Approach to Self-government*. Cambridge, 1956.

―――― *The Law and the Constitution*. 5th ed. London, 1963.

Johnston, B. F., and J. W. Melling. The Role of Agriculture in Economic Development. *American Economic Review*. September 1961.

Kelsen, H. *General Theory of Law and State*. Translated by A. Wedberg. New York, 1961.

Kindelberger, C. P. *Economic Development*, New York, 1965.

Lauterpacht, H. *Private Law Sources and Analogies of International Law*, 1927.

Lawson, F. H. *Introduction to the Law of Property*. Oxford, 1958.

League, R. W. *Roman Private Law*. London, 1962.

Leighton, A. H. *Human Relations in a Changing World*. New York, 1949.

Lerner, D., and W. Schramm. *Communications and Change in the Developing Countries*. Honolulu, 1967.

Lewis, O. *In a Mexican Village*. Urbana, Ill., 1951.

Lewis, W. A. *The Principles of Economic Planning*. London, 1950.

Liebenstein, H. *Economic Theory and Organizational Analysis.* New York, 1960.

Lindblom, C. E. The Science of Muddling Through. *Public Administration Review,* XIX (Spring 1959).

Llewellyn, K. N., and E. A. Hoebel. *The Cheyenne Way,* Norman, Okla., 1941.

Maine, Sir Henry S. *Ancient Law.* London, 1931.

Mair, P. *Studies in Applied Anthropology.* London, 1957.

Maitland, R. W. *The Constitutional History of England.* Cambridge, 1961.

Malinowski, B. *Argonauts of the Western Pacific.* New York, 1922.

—— *Crime and Custom in Savage Society.* London, 1926.

—— *The Sexual Life of Savages.* London, 1932.

—— Introduction to H. I. Hogbin, *Law and Order in Polynesia.* 1934.

—— A New Instrument for Interpretation of Law—Especially Primitive. *The Yale Law Review,* LI (1942).

Marshall, A. *Principles of Economics.* London, 1924.

Mangin, W. Haciendas, Comunidades and Strategic Acculturation in the Peruvian Sierra. *Sociologus,* N. S., VII, no. 2 (1957).

Meek, C. K. *Law and Authority in a Nigerian Tribe.* London, 1937.

Megarry, R. E. *A Manual of the Law of Real Property.* London, 1962.

Merton, R. K. The Role of Applied Social Science in the Formation of Policy. *Philosophy of Science,* XVI (July 1949).

Methods of Study of Culture Contact in Africa. Memorandum XV of the International Institute of African Languages and Cultures. 1938.

Mills, C. W. *The Sociological Imagination.* New York, 1959.

Mises, Ludwig von. *Omnipotent Government.* New Haven, 1944.

Myint, H. An Interpretation of Economic Backwardness. *Oxford Economic Papers.* June 1954.

Nadel, S. F. *The Foundations of Social Anthropology.* London, 1951.

Nash, M. The Multiple Society in Economic Development: Mexico and Guatemala. *American Anthropologist,* LIX (1959).

Niehoff, A. H. *A Casebook of Social Change.* Chicago, 1963.

Novack, D. E., and R. Lekachman. eds. *Development and Society.* New York, 1964.

Nurkse, R. *Patterns of Trade and Development.* Stockholm, 1959.

Paul, B. D., ed. *Health, Culture and Community.* New York, 1955.

Pearsall, M. Review of W. H. Goodenough's *Cooperation in Change,* in *Social Forces,* XLIII (1964).

Perham, M. *The Colonial Reckoning.* New York, 1962.

Philips, O. Hood. The Making of a Colonial Constitution. F1, *Law Quarterly Review*. 1955.

Pirenne, H. *Medieval Cities*. Princeton, 1923.

Polanyi, K. Anthropology and Economic Theory. In *Readings in Anthropology II*. Edited by M. H. Fried. New York, 1959.

Popper, K. R. *The Poverty of Historicism*. New York, 1964.

Pospisil, L. *Kapaukau Papuans and Their Law*. New Haven, 1959.

—— A Formal Analysis of Substantive Law; Kapaukau Papuan Laws of Inheritance. *AA*. Special Publication, 1965.

—— Law and Order, in *Introduction to Cultural Anthropology*. Edited by J. A. Clifton. Boston, 1968.

Potter, P. P. *An Introduction to the Study of International Organization*. New York, 1948.

Pound, R. *The Ideal Element in Law*. Calcutta, 1958.

Radcliffe-Brown, A. R. *Structure and Function in Primitive Society*. Glencoe, 1952.

Ranis, G., ed. *The United States and the Developing Economies*. New York, 1964.

Raup, P. M. The Contribution of Land Reforms to Economic Development. *Economic Development and Cultural Change*. October 1963.

Redfield, R. *The Primitive World and Its Transformation*. Ithaca, N.Y., 1953.

Riesman, D. *The Lonely Crowd*. New Haven, 1950.

Riggs, F. *Administration in Developing Countries*. Boston, 1964.

Rosovsky, H. and K. Ohkawa. The Role of Agriculture in Modern Japanese Economic Development. *Economic Development and Cultural Change*, IX, no. 1, Pt. II (October 1960).

Salisbury, R. F. *From Stone to Steel*. Cambridge, Eng., 1962.

—— Economic Anthropology: Retrospect and Prospect in E. E. LeClair and H. K. Schneider, *Economic Anthropology*. New York, 1968.

Salmond, Sir John. *Salmond on Jurisprudence*. London, 1957.

Say, J. B. *Treatise on Political Economy*. Boston, 1824.

Schapera, I. *A Handbook of Tawana Law and Custom*. London, 1938, 1955.

Schneider, H. K., and E. LeClair, Jr. (eds.). *Economic Anthropology*. New York, 1968.

Schramm, W. L. *The Process and Effects of Mass Communication*. Urbana, Ill., 1965.

Sharp, W. R. *National Administration and International Organization*. Brussels, 1951.

Shostack, A. B., ed. *Sociology in Action*. Homewood, Ill., 1966.

Silving, H. *Constituent Elements of Crime.* Springfield, Ill., 1967.

Simpson, A. W. B. The Analysis of Legal Concepts. *Law Quarterly Review,* LXXX (1964).

Sjoberg, G., ed. *Ethics, Politics and Social Research.* Cambridge, 1967.

Spicer, E. H., ed. *Human Problems in Technological Change.* New York, 1965.

Tax, S. The Uses of Anthropology. *In* J. D. Jennings and E. A. Hoebel, *Readings in Anthropology.* New York, 1966.

Theodorsen, G. A. Acceptance of Industrialization and Its Attendant Consequences for the Social Patterns of Non-Western Societies. *American Sociological Review,* XVIII (1953).

Thompson, L. Is Applied Anthropology Helping to Develop a Science of Man? *Human Organization,* XXIV (1965).

Thurnwald, R. Price of the White Man's Peace. *Pacific Affairs,* IX, no. 3.

Trevelyn, G. M. *English Social History.* 1942.

Turner, J. W. G., ed. *Kennys Outlines of Criminal Law.* Cambridge, 1966.

Twining, W. The Works of Karl Llewellyn. *The Modern Law Review,* XXXI (March 1968).

Waterston, A. *Development Planning: The Lessons of Experience.* Baltimore, 1965.

Weber, M. *The Theory of Social and Economic Organization.* Translated and edited by Talcott Parsons. New York, 1964.

Whitehead, A. N. *Adventures in Ideas.* New York, 1967.

Wilson, G. Anthropology as a Public Service. *Africa,* XIII (1940).

Wilson, J. S. G. *An Economic Survey of the New Hebrides.* London, 1965.

Winch, P. *The Idea of a Social Science and Its Relation to Philosophy.* London, 1968.

Worsley, P. Bureaucracy and Decolonization. *The New Sociology.* Edited by I. L. Horowitz. New York, 1964.

Index